SOMETHING FOR NOTHING?

OS JUSTI STUDIES IN CATHOLIC TRADITION
General Editor: Peter A. Kwasniewski

1 ✦ J. Joy, *Disputed Questions on Papal Infallibility*

2 ✦ R.-M. Rivoire, *Does "Traditionis Custodes" Pass the Juridical Rationality Test?*

3 ✦ J. Shaw, *The Liturgy, the Family, and the Crisis of Modernity*

4 ✦ P. Kwasniewski (ed.), *Illusions of Reform*

5 ✦ G. Steckler, *The Triumph of Romanticism*

6 ✦ T. Crean, *"Letters from that City . . .": A Guide to Holy Scripture for Students of Theology*

7 ✦ S. Lanzetta, *God's Abode with Man: The Mystery of Divine Grace*

8 ✦ A. Fimister, *The Iron Sceptre of the Son of Man*

9 ✦ S. Lanzetta, *"Super Hanc Petram": The Pope and the Church at a Dramatic Moment in History*

10 ✦ P. Kwasniewski (ed.), *Ultramontanism and Tradition*

11 ✦ U. Hannon, *Thomistic Mystagogy*

12 ✦ A. Thornton-Norris, *The Spiritual History of English*

13 ✦ P. Kwasniewski (ed.), *Unresolved Tensions in the Papal-Episcopal Relationship*

14 ✦ D. Hunt, *Something for Nothing?*

Something for Nothing?

*An Explanation and Defence
of the
Scholastic Position on Usury*

DAVID HUNT

OS JUSTI PRESS

LINCOLN, NEBRASKA

Copyright © 2024 by Os Justi Press
All rights reserved.

No part of this book may be reproduced, stored in a retrieval system, or transmitted in any form, or by any means, electronic, mechanical, photocopying, or otherwise, without the prior written permission of the publisher, except by a reviewer, who may quote brief passages in a review.

Os Justi Press
P.O. Box 21814
Lincoln, NE 68542
www.osjustipress.com

Send inquiries to
info@osjustipress.com

ISBN 978-1-965303-01-6 (paperback)
ISBN 978-1-965303-02-3 (hardcover)
ISBN 978-1-965303-03-0 (ebook)

Typesetting by Michael Schrauzer
Cover design by Julian Kwasniewski
Detail from Evelyn De Morgan, *Earthbound* (1897)
Wikimedia Commons

For Katie Rose, Felicity, Theresa,
Joseph, Maria, Anna and Clare

We exhort you not to listen to those who say that today the issue of usury is present in name only, since gain is almost always obtained from money given to another. How false is this opinion and how far removed from the truth! We can easily understand this if we consider that the nature of one contract differs from the nature of another.
Benedict XIV, *Vix Pervenit*

The mischief has been increased by rapacious usury, which, although more than once condemned by the Church, is nevertheless, under a different guise, but with like injustice, still practiced by covetous and grasping men.
Leo XIII, *Rerum Novarum*

What is more, nothing makes property run into a few hands but the worst of the capital sins, and you who say it is "the modern facility of distribution"... are like men who should say that their drunkenness was due to their drink, or that arson was caused by matches.
Hilaire Belloc

For definitions are very dreadful things: they do the two things that most men, especially comfortable men, cannot endure. They fight; and they fight fair.
G. K. Chesterton

CONTENTS

Acknowledgements xi

Glossary xii

Introduction 1

1 What Is Usury? 13
  1.1 The *mutuum* as a Roman contract 13
  1.2 Aquinas on use and ownership in a *mutuum* 15
    1.2.1 Use consuming 16
    1.2.2 Double-charging or selling what doesn't exist 20
    1.2.3 Personal guarantees 21
  1.3 The fixed value of fungibles 23
  1.4 Extrinsic titles: the case for damages 27
  1.5 Two other arguments against usury 33

2 Can Interest be Charged for Other Things Besides the Use of Money? 38
  2.1 Counterarguments rooted in a *mutuum* 41
  2.2 A transitional debate 44
  2.3 The economic justification 46
    2.3.1 Interest as equalising time preference 48
    2.3.2 Risk 50
    2.3.3 Inflation 52

3 If Interest Can Never be Charged, What Course of Action Is Left? 55
  3.1 The *societas* or partnership 55
  3.2 The *census* or contract of rent 59
  3.3 The triple contract 65

4 Does Usury Really Deserve Our Attention? 70
  4.1 Interest on a *mutuum* implies the borrower is the lender's property 70
  4.2 Distinguishing two forms of slavery 72
  4.3 Usury as financial chattel slavery 75

Appendices 79
   1. *Institutes* 81
   2. *Summa Theologiae*: The sin of usury 85
   3. Decrees of the Council of Vienne 109
   4. *Regimini Universalis* 111
   5. *Inter Multiplices* 113
   6. *Cum Onus* 114
   7. Various Errors on Moral Subjects 117
   8. *Vix Pervenit* 118

Bibliography 125

ACKNOWLEDGEMENTS

THERE are many people who have contributed, in some small way, to the ideas in this book, having entertained conversation on the topic over the last decade.

More notable thanks must, in the first place, go to my parents. Were it not for their generosity and support in the Summer of 2013, I would never have been able to study at the International Theological Institute in Austria which led, eleven years later, to this book. I owe enormous thanks to Dr. Alan Fimister on a few fronts: firstly, for his classes in Austria where I first came across usury; secondly, for hours of discussion on this and every other topic, which were not only reliably informative, but also inspiring; and thirdly, for his involvement in the publication of this work. The McKinnons and Robert Cassidy have provided invaluable advice along the way, as well as generous hospitality over the years. There are many aspects of this book which are much more readable because of their advice and criticism.

Special thanks must also go to Peter Kwasniewski for his careful suggestions and editorial advice, which have made the book more accurate and more readable.

Lastly, to Katie Rose. Thank you.

GLOSSARY

Mutuum — i. the loan of such things as are estimated by weight, number or measure — for instance, wine, oil, corn, coined money, copper, silver or gold: things in which we transfer our property on condition that the receiver shall transfer to us, at a future time, not the same things, but other things of the same kind and quality;[1] ii. the loan of a good treated as fungible in which the borrower promises (personally guarantees) to repay the debt in kind, not in particular.

Usury — i. anything received above the principal on a *mutuum* by virtue of the loan itself; ii. profitable interest on personally guaranteed recourse lending to an individual.

✦ ✦ ✦

Alienate — to transfer ownership of a particular piece of property to another.

Census — "a contract of purchase of the right to receive an annual payment from some property or person."[2]

Contract — "a mutual agreement concerning the transfer of a right."[3]

Fungible — interchangeable for use, replaceable by another identical item.

Extrinsic titles — "titles which are not at all intrinsic to the contract ... from [which] ... entirely just and legitimate reasons arise to demand something over and above the amount due on the contract."[4]

---

[1] "Re contrahitur obligatio veluti mutui datione. mutui autem obligatio in his rebus consistit, quae pondere numero mensurave constant, veluti vino oleo frumento pecunia numerata aere argento auro, quas res aut numerando aut metiendo aut pendendo in hoc damus, ut accipientium fiant et quandoque nobis non eaedem res, sed aliae eiusdem naturae et qualitatis reddantur." Justinian, *Imperatoris Iustiniani Institutionum, Libri Quattuor*, ed. J. B. Moyle, 4th ed. (Oxford: Clarendon Press, 1903), 392.

[2] Bernard W. Dempsey, *Interest and Usury* (London: Dobson, 1948), 161.

[3] Austin Fagothey, *Right and Reason: Ethics in Theory and Practice*, 4th ed. (St. Louis: C. V. Mosby, 1967), 336.

[4] Benedict XIV, *Vix Pervenit*, 1745, par. 9 of 20, www.papalencyclicals.net/ben14/b14vixpe.htm.

Glossary

Insurance — a pooling of financial assets such that they can be used to cover the insured parties' costs in the case that a specific set of events actually occurs.

Interest — the numerical difference between the principal and repayment on a loan.

Ownership — "the right of exclusive control and disposal over a thing at will."[5]

Personal guarantee — a promise of the borrower to repay the loan entailing a personal liability which gives the lender recourse to the borrower and the borrower's assets to recoup anything owed.

Principal — the amount borrowed in a loan contract (*mutuum* or any other type of loan).

Profitable interest — interest on a loan without a legitimate title.

Property — that which is owned.

Security — some specified set of assets that are pledged as collateral in a contract and guarantee that the contracting parties fulfil their obligations.

Societas — a type of investment contract, also known as a partnership agreement. An agreement made between an investor and a merchant, in which the investor committed money, the merchant labour, and together the two partners share the profits of the venture.

Title — a bundle of rights in a particular piece of property.

Triple contract — a bundle of three contracts used by investors and merchants. The first is a *societas*. The second is an insurance contract on the principal provided by the merchant to the investor, guaranteeing its return. The third contract is an insurance contract on a fixed return.

---

[5] Fagothey, *Right and Reason*, 368.

INTRODUCTION

Almost everything written or said about usury today is based on a misunderstanding. Usury today is considered to be the charging of excessive interest on loans, rather than the supposedly outmoded (and some would say outrageous) definition of usury as the charging of any interest on a loan. While it would be quite foolish in the eyes of many to make any attempt to defend the older position, its very existence continues to raise (at least for those who look for it) the problem of the internal consistency and continuity of the Catholic Church's teaching. To avoid or minimise this dilemma, some argue for a "development" of Church doctrine. Others maintain that Church doctrine has simply changed and are quite happy with that conclusion. Still others tie themselves in knots attempting to solve the conundrum.

Writing in the thirteenth century, St. Thomas Aquinas, with characteristic precision, presents the essential argument against usury. This argument situates usury exclusively in a specific loan contract, a *mutuum*, concluding that usury is a charge for something that does not exist and is therefore theft.

All things can be divided into two categories: things that *are* used up in their use, and things that *are not* used up in their use. For those things that are used up in their use, like food, wine, and medicine, the use cannot be separated from ownership. It would be ridiculous for someone to sell you a bottle of wine, but then say, "and if you use the wine, then you will owe me something extra." The person who owns the thing also has the right to the use of the thing, which is its consumption. To attempt to sell the thing and introduce an additional charge for its use would be to sell something that doesn't exist: the use of the thing separate from ownership. Selling something that doesn't exist is theft, despite what some Austrian economists might argue.

For those things that are not used up or consumed in their use, such as houses or cars, ownership and use are separable. The owner of a house can retain ownership, but let another use the house for a period of time. It is morally licit for individuals to make a profit by the use of their own property, and therefore charging rent is a legitimate profit-making venture.

Money falls into the first category of goods, in that it is used up or consumed in its use. If you use your money by giving it in a loan, then you no longer have that money. The Scholastics maintained that charging interest for such a loan, something over and above the principal, is contrary to justice, which demands an equivalence in exchange.

STRUCTURE OF THIS WORK

This book is structured around four simple questions reflecting a pattern that I have come to see repeated in conversation after conversation on usury and interest. The first question is: what is usury? The second: can interest be charged for anything besides the use of money? The third: if interest can never be charged, then what course of action is left? And the fourth: does usury really deserve our attention?

What is usury? The first step is to define the only contract in which usury occurs, the *mutuum*. Once the definition is established, it will be clear how and why it relates to personally guaranteed loans of things that are used up in their use. Examples of such goods are wine or bread, which do not exist in the same sense once they have been used. It is critical to see, in this context, how the concepts of use and ownership apply to a *mutuum*.

The discussion requires that one consider whether it is justifiable to sell something that does not exist. On the basis of the view that this is a species of theft, it is essential to look at the way in which one can determine the value of the sorts of goods under discussion.

There are also a limited number of scenarios in which the Scholastics permitted charges on a loan (*mutuum*) of money. These come under the heading of "extrinsic titles" and will be looked at next. Finally in this chapter, two other arguments against usury will be discussed to highlight two important distinctions and clear the way for the remaining discussion.

Can interest be charged for anything besides the use of money? Since the Scholastic position prohibits charging interest for the use of money in a *mutuum*, it is necessary to consider whether there are other things which could be the source of interest. This question requires the arguments of late Scholastic contributors and economists from the eighteenth century onwards. In brief, these include arguments for time preference, risk (including the nature of insurance), or inflation giving rise to just ground for interest.

It will also be instructive to note briefly how usury in common parlance shifted from being *any* interest (the Scholastic position) to *excessive* interest (the Modern position). The discussion of usury and interest between Adam Smith and Jeremy Bentham is the definitive point in this transition.

If interest can never be charged, what course of action is left? Many assume that a prohibition on usury touches every credit transaction in the economy. This is not the case. The Scholastic discussion analysed numerous other contracts which enabled many forms of enterprise and profit-seeking without committing usury. Looking at these contracts permits important distinctions between full and limited recourse lending in a whole range of commercial activities which are perfectly legitimate when considered in light of the arguments against usury.

In order to answer this question, the discussion on risk and insurance will be revisited, as it influenced, in the late Middle Ages, contract innovation for the purpose of avoiding usury.

Does usury really deserve our attention? Finally, since many well-intentioned people argue that the Church has changed her teaching or that the nature of economic activity itself has changed, rendering the concept of usury devoid of all substance, it is necessary to analyse more closely the problems that usury entails. One is that usury is in the same moral genus as slavery. Charging interest on a *mutuum* is an attempt to profit by treating the borrower as the property of the lender and as such is a form of chattel slavery.

RATIONALE FOR THIS WORK

From the thirteenth to the twenty-first centuries, the common understanding of usury changed beyond recognition. The Scholastic position, the moral prohibition on receiving back anything over and above the principal on personally guaranteed *mutuum* loans, persisted until the end of the seventeenth century. It had developed organically, adapting to the growing and developing economies of Europe during late Antiquity, through the high Middle Ages and into the early Modern period. This understanding had changed entirely by the eighteenth century, when the discussion shifted to the legitimacy of legal maximums for interest in loans of money. In other words, the discussion around it hinged on a by-then accepted—but previously rigorously denied—concept of the "fruitfulness" of money.

This shift in understanding and in the basic philosophical presuppositions is so significant that it becomes extremely difficult to bring the two sides into constructive discussion. To illustrate this point, take Leonardus Lessius (1554–1623), a Flemish Jesuit, theologian, philosopher, and contributor to the usury debate, writing in the fifteenth century about money in the context of the discussion on usury: "Money can neither be a commodity, or be sold as a commodity, except on the basis of its material or on a circumstance extrinsic to its nature."[6] By contrast, Anne Jacques Turgot, a French aristocrat and hero of Austrian and Libertarian economists, claims that "it is essential that money [be] considered in commerce as a genuine commodity whose price depends

---

[6] Leonardus Lessius, *On Sale, Securities, and Insurance*, trans. Wim Decock and Nicholas De Sutter (Grand Rapids, MI: CLP Academic, 2016), Book 2, chapter 21, part 2.1.

on agreement and varies, like that of all other commodities, according to the ratio between offer and demand."[7] Similarly, compare the Aristotelian analysis of money, which asserts categorically that money is sterile, with Adam Smith's view that "as something can everywhere be made by the use of money, something ought everywhere to be paid for the use of it."[8] These are just two examples of the depth of the divide between the two sides of a centuries-long discussion.

John T. Noonan, in his seminal mid-twentieth-century work *The Scholastic Analysis of Usury*, attempts to have the last say on the matter for the Modernist camp. Noonan claims that "usury today is a dead issue and except by a plainly equivocal use of the term, or save in the mouths of a few inveterate haters of the present order, it is not likely to stir to life."[9] This general sentiment has not since improved; the topic has been all but buried rather than adequately recalled, defined, clarified, and understood.

In contrast to Noonan, it would be more accurate to say that *usury is a thoroughly misunderstood issue*. Because of this misunderstanding, it is dismissed as irrelevant or insignificant—the Church changed her teaching but what does that matter; usury may have been relevant in the medieval economy, but in the modern economy it is merely an empty concept, a theoretical anachronism.

Despite Noonan's confidence, not all important twentieth-century thinkers have been led by common opinion. Hilaire Belloc, for instance, made two notable contributions to the debate. First, he took the Scholastic prohibition on usury seriously and saw in it an abiding relevance for today. Second, recognising a difficulty in rendering

---

[7] Anne Robert Jacques Turgot, *The Turgot Collection: Writings, Speeches, and Letters of Anne Robert Jacques Turgot*, ed. Gordon David (Auburn, AL: Ludwig von Mises Institute, 2011), 210.
[8] Adam Smith, *The Wealth of Nations* (Middlesex, England: Penguin Books Ltd, 1982), 456.
[9] John T. Noonan, *The Scholastic Analysis of Usury* (Cambridge, MA: Harvard University Press, 1957), 12. This book is one of the most quoted works in contemporary usury discussions.

the topic accessible, Belloc developed the theory, making a distinction between productive and unproductive loans to rehabilitate an understanding of usury.[10] Unfortunately, his argument can be rebutted quite succinctly, since there are situations in which one could enter into a *mutuum* with someone who uses the loan for productive purposes. The Scholastics levelled their arguments against interest on a *mutuum* irrespective of the purpose to which the funds were put once the loan began.

To return to an authentic understanding of usury, a light must be shone on three sources of obscurity, three challenges which contribute to the confusion that mark this complex and crucial topic. The first is a problem of translation, the second is a problem of distinctions, the third difficulty arises as a result of usury spanning many disciplines.

The problem of translation is the most common, but once seen, easy to recognise again and again. Take the following passages: "The nature of the sin called usury has its proper place and origin in a loan contract."[11] Or: "I answer that to take usury for money lent is unjust in itself."[12] Again:

> If thou hast lent thy money on usury to man, that is, if thou hast given the loan of thy money to one, from whom thou dost expect to receive something more than thou hast given, not in money only, but anything, whether it be wheat, or wine, or oil, or whatever else you please, if you expect to receive more than you have given, you are an usurer, and in this particular are not deserving of praise, but of censure.[13]

---

[10] Belloc was not the only writer to make this distinction; it can be found in germ as early as Calvin, and explicitly formulated by Cardinal de la Luzerne in 1822. Contemporary legal scholar Brian McCall supports the same distinction, albeit with minor modifications.
[11] Benedict XIV, *Vix Pervenit*.
[12] Thomas Aquinas, *Summa Theologiae: Secunda Secundae, 1–91*, trans. Fr. Laurence Shapcote, O. P. (Lander, Wyoming: The Aquinas Institute for the Study of Sacred Doctrine, 2012), q78, a1, resp.
[13] St. Augustine, *Nicene and Post-Nicene Fathers*, vol. 8, ed. Philip Schaff, Christian Classics Ethereal Library, Series I (Grand Rapids,

These passages and hundreds of others have one thing in common, that the term "loan" (or "lend") are English translations of the Latin term *mutuum*. The most likely etymology is from *mutare*: to change, to exchange. In English, "loan" does not refer to any particular type of thing lent, but is a general term. The natural law argument against usury arises solely in the context of lending under a *mutuum*. The distinct nature of this contract, *as opposed to other forms of lending, be that in rents or secured lending*, is fundamental. It is ubiquitous in the Scholastic school of thought on usury but largely absent from discussion of usury since the eighteenth century. Knowing that *mutua* ought to be present in any discussion of usury is the antidote to the first difficulty.

Once the potential for a *mutuum* to lie behind any discussion on usury is recognised, the second difficulty, that of distinction, comes more plainly into view. If a *mutuum* is one form of contract that is translated into English as loan, what are the other contracts that also translate as loan? And what is it that makes a *mutuum* distinct from other sorts of contracts?

One way to define a contract is an agreement creating an obligation for the consenting parties. Fortunately, in the ordinary course of events it is not something one has to think about at all. Getting a taxi, buying milk from the supermarket, going to work, renting a house all involve a contract of some form, each explicit to a greater or lesser degree. Aquinas uncovers this point in his discussion of usury by contrasting a good used up in its use to a good not used up in its use. Compare wine to a car: the wine is drunk and therefore used up in its use; the car is driven but not used up in its use. The difference between these two examples highlights two aspects which need to be seen and understood in tandem: the agreement and the nature of the object of the agreement.

This distinction and appreciation of the sort of agreement and contract at issue has the effect of clarifying and

---

MI: Christian Classics Ethereal Library, n.d.), 210.

narrowing the scope of discussion on usury. It very rapidly does away with the broad and all-encompassing view that usury is "any interest on a loan." For a loan could be the result of encumbering one's land or farm, in which case the question of ownership pertains to the underlying land or farm, an immobile good, not to money as such. Alternatively, the loan could be to a legal entity which is administered by others, and the interplay of the thing loaned and the type of agreement created gives rise to a set of obligations distinct from those in a *mutuum*. When these alternative types of loans or investments are considered alongside a *mutuum*, and the different facets of the agreements considered, clear principles can be drawn out which differentiate one from another.

The third difficulty is born of the fact that usury is a topic which crosses the boundaries of many disciplines. The main arguments against usury were developed under the premises of Scholastic philosophy. Aquinas synthesised the discussion on usury that preceded him and fastened the debate to secure moorings with an argument that illuminated the essence of the issue. His account became the standard for subsequent centuries, and, although complemented and developed, remained the centre of gravity for any understanding of usury. As the Enlightenment project took over and modern philosophy gradually supplanted medieval philosophy, Aquinas's argument was not rebutted; it was simply ignored. As the general method of philosophy changed, so too did every area in which usury could be considered: justice, morals, economics. Any grasp of what had once been authoritative was lost to the common consciousness.

Amid the relative unity of Church and state throughout the Middle Ages, there were powerful mechanisms to translate the discussions of theologians into practical aids to guide moral questions. This happened principally through the confessional, where, amongst other consequences, unrepentant usurers faced the denial of Christian burial. This cultural and psychological reality is not to be underestimated in containing the potential for avarice. The ecclesial and civil courts in England, for instance, adjudicated many cases of contractual matters where usury was suspected but not obvious.[14] These private judgements in the confessional and public judgements in the courts checked the spread of usury. With the separation of the Church and state following the complex of developments called the Protestant Revolt or Reformation, these cultural forces began to break down. In particular, as wealth and earthly success became a visible sign of predestination in Protestantism, the whole cultural gamut no longer favoured a careful and balanced view of justice in contracts.

This is borne out in the philosophy of the early Protestant thinkers, where, in practical matters pertaining to usury, sound philosophy was replaced by personal authority in matters of economics and justice. "It could be wished that all usury and the name itself were first banished from the earth. But as this cannot be accomplished it should be seen what can be done for the public good."[15] However the rules then put forward "for the public good" are not grounded in natural law and perennial philosophy, nor supported by the weight of teaching from an authority (i.e., the Catholic Church). Rather, the preferred new approach entailed the priority of the personal opinion of Protestant leaders themselves. Once this unmooring from sound foundations had begun, the stage was set for the topic to move where the wind blows.

The repositioning of theology undertaken by the early Protestant thinkers also flowed into the legal sphere. The Protestant movement emphasises a conception of the legal process which begins to favour the expediency of bare

---

[14] R. H. Helmolz, "Usury and the Medieval English Church Courts," *Speculum* 61, no. 2 (1986): 364–80.
[15] John Calvin, *Letter of Calvin: De Usuris Responsum*, printed in Calvin Elliot, *Usury: A Scriptural, Ethical and Economic View* (n.p.: Aeterna Publishing, 2010), 38–40.

agreements over moral and ethical practices grounded in the natural law. This is coupled with the success of the scientific method applied to economic science, which reduces human relationships and bonds to mere calculations. The result is the primacy of agreement and consent for subjective gain rather than sound moral and legal principles adapted to the exigencies of everyday life.

These themes of theology, philosophy, economics, and law played out over hundreds of years. Down through the centuries, the increase in factors to consider rendered the arguments harder to penetrate. Without recognising these obscuring factors, and digging deeper, it had become plausible to maintain—and continues to be plausible—that usury was no longer *all* interest on loans but only *excessive* interest. The simplifying fiction that economic realities have fundamentally changed, and therefore we can no longer speak of usury in the same way as was intended 800 years ago, while fatally flawed, becomes a comforting solution.

Against this backdrop, this book aims to show that *essential to usury is the idea of recourse in contracts*. Where there is recourse to assets distinct from the contracting parties, this points away from a *mutuum*. Interest in this context may or may not be justified, legitimate, and moral, but it is not usury. A personal guarantee and recourse to the borrower implies a *mutuum*. Profitable interest in this context is usury. Aquinas's argument begins with the simple distinction between things used up in their use and things not used up in their use. This book takes the first division and extends the argument in terms of recourse, to make this often opaque topic clearer, while maintaining the substance of the Scholastic analysis. The idea of recourse does not at first appear as central in the history of usury and its related arguments. It is only with hindsight that the contributions and arguments can be pieced together to rehabilitate the overall argument against usury.

This work therefore is a defence and development of the Scholastic position on usury: *Personally guaranteed recourse lending to an individual for profitable interest is always usury and morally unjustifiable. Limited recourse lending for interest secured by collateral is not usurious, though it may involve other ethical implications.* I hope in this way to move the discussion on usury to a stronger foundation.

One need not look far to find hastily scribbled hit-pieces or think-tank-funded *precis* that glibly or superficially consign centuries of philosophical, legal, and economic thought to the scrap heap. There is more to recover than a sound grasp of arguments against usury. On the one hand, the modern account of usury is a straw man masking a real and pervasive evil; on the other, the idea that eradicating usury is the panacea that will recover sound ethical economics is also false. Defining what usury is and is not, and identifying where it exists, is an indispensable beginning.

I
WHAT IS USURY?

1.1 THE *MUTUUM* AS A ROMAN CONTRACT

Usury has been a source of complex debate for centuries. There are very many facets to the topic that, after centuries of back and forth, have become obscured or are now emphasised less than others. Understanding usury can begin only by considering the "nature of how one contract differs from another."[1] Without this initial work of distinguishing how contractual agreements fundamentally differ from one another, any attempt to understand the historic debate on usury will fail. The Scholastic analysis of usury is founded on the contract of the *mutuum*. "*Usura solum in mutuo cadit*" (usury only falls in a loan [*mutuum*].)[2] "*Usura non gignitur materialiter nisi de mutuo*"[3] (usury arises only in a *mutuum*). It is only in this type of contract that usury can be found, so it is essential to define the contract and distinguish it from alternatives.

In the broadest terms, a contract is "a practical, external manifestation of one to another generating an obligation from the consent of the parties agreeing."[4] This definition implies that contracts are an implicit and ubiquitous facet of life: one enters into very many contracts in the course of everyday life. Not only for those things where

---

[1] Benedict XIV, *Vix Pervenit*, par. 18.
[2] San Bernardino, *De Evangelio Aeterno*, sermon 36, art. 1, cap. 1 and 2, art. 2, cap. 1, 2, and 3 and sermon 37, art. 1, cap. 2 (*Opera omnia*, IV, 205, 207-209, 224-25) cited in Raymond de Roover, *San Bernardino of Siena and Saint Antonino of Florence: The Two Great Economic Thinkers of the Middle Ages*, The Kress Library of Business and Economics 19 (Boston: Baker Library, 1967), 28.
[3] Lawrin D. Armstrong, *The Idea of a Moral Economy: Gerard of Siena on Usury, Restitution, and Prescription* (Toronto: Toronto University Press, 2016), 52.
[4] Leonardus Lessius, *De Iustitia et Iure*, 17: 1–4, 16 sq. cited in Dempsey, *Interest and Usury*, 140.

one physically signs an agreement, but down to the smallest act, like buying milk.

The contractual concepts that serve as the foundation for the Scholastic discussion on usury are derived from Roman law. The main division of contracts is described by Leonardus Lessius:

> A named contract is one which has a special and proper name by which it is distinguished from others, as purchase, sale, loan (*mutuum*), hire (*locatio*), association (*societas*), loan of accommodation (*commodatum*), pledge or mortgage (*pignus*), deposit (*depositum*), and the like. An unnamed contract has no special name but only the generic one.[5]

These are named contracts because the law expressly defines their terms and requirements, as opposed to unnamed contracts which are not explicitly named in civil codes but are simply constituted on the agreement of the parties and their own terms. These four named contracts — the *mutuum*, the *commodatum*, the *depositum*, and the *pignus* — are found in Book XIV of Justinian's *Institutes*, compiled in the sixth century. The *Institutes*' definition of a *mutuum* runs as follows:

> The loan [*mutuum*] of such things as are estimated by weight, number or measure, for instance, wine, oil, corn, coined money, copper, silver or gold: things in which we transfer our property on condition that the receiver shall transfer to us, at a future time, not the same things, but other things of the same kind and quality.[6]

Two concepts need to be noted here. The first, that "we transfer our property" leading to Justinian's poetic etymology of *mutuum*: "*meum* or mine, becomes *tuum* or thine."[7] The second, that the loan entails "not the same things but other things of the same kind and quality" be returned.

---
[5] Ibid.
[6] Justinian, *The Institutes of Justinian*, ed. Moyle, J. B., 4th ed. (Oxford: Clarendon Press, 1913), 130.
[7] Justinian, 130.

Phrased another way, the borrower in a *mutuum* returns the goods *in kind*, not *in particular*. This can be seen by considering the distinction between a *commodatum* and a *mutuum*. In the first (e.g., the loan of a car) the goods endure through use and can be returned in particular. In the second (e.g., the loan of wine) the goods are used up and only returned in kind.

1.2 AQUINAS ON USE AND OWNERSHIP IN A *MUTUUM*

Thomas Aquinas is the most prominent figure in the usury debate for his formulation of the perennial argument against usury. Noonan not only divides the periods of development as "before and after" Aquinas, but asserts that "St. Thomas holds a special place in the development of the usury theory; and the importance of his opinions cannot easily be exaggerated."[8] Aquinas treats usury in at least three works: the *Commentary on the Sentences* of Peter Lombard which forms part of Aquinas's early work; his treatise *De Malo* (*On Evil*); and the economic questions in the *Summa Theologiae*.

The argument of Aquinas's later works, which becomes the defining formulation in the argument against usury of the Scholastic period, is contained in *De Malo*. It synthesises Aristotelian ideas and the Roman law concept of the *mutuum*. The argument runs as follows:

> We should consider that there are different uses of different things. For there are some things whose use consists of consuming the things themselves. For example, the proper use of wine consists in drinking it, and the substance of the wine is thereby consumed, and the proper use of wheat or bread likewise consists of eating it, and this consumes the wheat or bread itself...
>
> And there are some things whose use does not consist of consuming the things themselves. For example, the use of a house is as a dwelling, and it does not belong to the nature of inhabitation

---

[8] Noonan, *The Scholastic Analysis of Usury*, 51.

that the house be razed... Therefore, since use does not consume such things, strictly speaking, the thing itself or its use can be separately leased or sold, or both together can be alienated. For example, one can sell a house while retaining one's use of the house for a time, and one can likewise sell the use of a house while retaining one's title and ownership of the house.

But regarding the things whose use consists of consuming them, *the use of the thing is only the thing itself,* and so whoever is granted the use of such things is also granted the ownership of the things themselves, and vice versa. Therefore, when a person lends money [i.e., in a *mutuum*] with the stipulation that the entire sum be returned, and the person in addition wants to have a fixed recompense for the use of the money, the person evidently sells separately the use of the money and the very substance of money. And the use of money is only its substance, as I have said, and so the lender of money at interest [*usura*] sells nothing or sells the same thing twice, namely, the very money whose use consists of its consumption, and this is evidently contrary to the nature of natural justice.[9]

There are two concepts to unpack in this argument. The first is the manner in which use and ownership are to be distinguished in different goods. The second is the conclusion that lending money at interest is to "sell nothing or sell the same thing twice."

1.2.1 Use consuming

Aquinas claims that "regarding the things whose use consists of consuming them, the use of the thing is only the thing itself." One could not reasonably talk of using wine or bread without this entailing the notion of the thing being gone once used. One might object and say this isn't strictly speaking

---

[9] Thomas Aquinas, *On Evil,* trans. Richard Regan (New York: Oxford University Press, 2003), q13, a4; emphasis added.

the case, as wine or bread could be used as a doorstop, or a paperweight or in some other similar way which does not consist in their consumption. Indeed, Aquinas draws on Aristotle's *Politics* to make the same distinction:

> Things can have two uses: one specific and primary; the other general and secondary. For example, the specific and primary use of shoes is to wear them, and their secondary use is to exchange them for something else. And conversely, the specific and primary use of money is as a means of exchange, since money was instituted for this purpose, and the secondary use of money can be for anything else, for example, as security or for display.[10]

In the case of our examples of wine and bread, while they can be used as doorstops and paperweights, these would be "general and secondary" uses, rather than "specific and primary." This permits an additional level of precision for the previous statement: one could not reasonably talk of using wine or bread *in their specific and primary sense* without this entailing the notion that the things will be gone once used. This makes plain the fact that in some class of goods use follows essentially from ownership and cannot be separated from it. Such goods are called fungible; settling a loan of such goods can only be done with other things of the same kind and quantity, not the same things. In contrast there is no difficulty in separating the use and ownership in such things as a house, as anyone who has ever rented a place to live will attest to.

To the point as to whether money is used up in its use or not, Juan de Molina (1485–1552), a late-Scholastic Jesuit theologian and philosopher, clarifies the meaning of consumption, saying: "the word consumption [with respect to the object of a *mutuum*] includes also the use of a thing by alienation; for which reason, when something is paid for with it, or it is exchanged for something else, or given away, or lent, it is said, with reference to the one giving it,

---

[10] Aquinas, *On Evil*, 400.

to be consumed, inasmuch as by such use the ownership of it passes to another."[11]

One can read this along the following lines: it is clear that once money has been used, i.e., spent in exchange, it still exists, which is categorically different from the case of wine and bread, which are gone. This gives rise to the question of whether money really is a thing consumed in its use since it is not the same as wine in this respect. However, Molina indicates that once money loaned in a *mutuum* has been used, despite still existing, the user no longer has any right to that money as his property. Its ownership has been transferred to another, so with respect to the borrower, the money is consumed. The fact that he may well have other property in place of the money is beside the point for present purposes. The manner in which this argument uses the word "consumed" is that the borrower no longer has the good once he has exercised ownership over it by using it.[12]

This concept of consumption can be further developed by considering how the nature of the contract changes when money is used in a "general and secondary" sense in a bailment (the act of delivering goods to a bailee for a particular purpose without transfer of ownership). This will also shed light on an important facet of a *mutuum* contract, namely that a *mutuum* treats the goods loaned as fungible.

All Scholastic authors consider the case of money lent in a bailment, or *ad pompam*. Such an agreement is typified by the loan of rare coins for display. In the case of the loan of money *ad pompam*, since the contract does not treat the money as fungible (that is, the money is treated according to a general and secondary purpose, not its primary and specific), it is no longer governed by the contract of a *mutuum*.[13] Aquinas argues:

---

[11] Molina, *De Justice et Jure*, cited in Dempsey, *Interest and Usury*, 143.
[12] This is also clarified if one take Aquinas's commentary: "exchange is a use consuming, as it were, the substance of the thing exchanged insofar as the exchange alienates the thing from the one who exchanges it." Aquinas, *On Evil*, 403.
[13] "Every... Scholastic writer accepts such a bailment of money in its secondary use as licit." Noonan, *The Scholastic Analysis of Usury*, 55.

> But if persons lend their money to others for another use in which the money is not consumed, there will be the same consideration as regarding the things that are not consumed in their very use, things that are licitly rented and hired out. And so if one gives money sealed in a purse to post it as security and then receives recompense, this is not interest-taking [usury], since it involves renting or hiring out, not a contract for a loan [*mutuum*].[14]

This should be clear since a *mutuum* entails that the borrower returns not the same but "other things of the same kind and quantity." The exact same coins are expected at the term of a bailment. The argument against usury does not apply because the contract is not a *mutuum* loan. There is no opposition to charging rent for the money loaned (*ad pompam*) even as one charges rent for the use of a house.

An important facet of the *mutuum* contract can now be illustrated, namely that a *mutuum* is a contract in which goods are treated as fungible. "A *mutuum* loan is not, strictly speaking, a loan of a fungible thing: it is a loan of a thing which the contract treats as fungible."[15] Money is treated as fungible in a *mutuum*, in contrast to a bailment in which money is not treated as fungible. This point will be important when investigating how personal guarantees follow from the nature of a *mutuum*.

---

[14] Aquinas, *On Evil*, q13, a4, ad15.
[15] Thomas Dickson, ed., *Usury: Frequently Asked Questions*, 3rd ed. (Saint Paul: Zippy, 2017), 34–45. On this point, Noonan (*The Scholastic Analysis of Usury*, 57) begs the question of whether Aquinas's argument is complete, in a short, almost throwaway section immediately after considering his main argument. Noonan's nonconsumptible fungibles, or "paperclip," objection can be countered with this fact: a *mutuum* treats the goods loaned as fungible, whether they are consumptible or not. If paperclips, or swatches of cloth, lead for ballast, young pink pigs, etc., are treated as fungible, then they are loaned under a *mutuum*, and the analysis applies. If they are not treated as fungible, there is no *mutuum*.

1.2.2 Double-charging or selling what doesn't exist

Aquinas's argument concludes: "so the lender of money at interest [*usura*] sells nothing or sells the same thing twice, namely, the very money whose use consists of its consumption."[16] What does this really mean? Firstly, lending money at interest in a *mutuum* means that the lender transfers ownership of a fixed sum to the borrower and expects the fixed sum, plus interest in return. The question Aquinas is trying to answer is: what is the basis of interest? Now this could either be a charge for the money itself, or for the use of the money. If it is for the money itself, returning the whole sum pays the debt and any interest attempts to charge for the same sum of money again, which is to sell the same thing twice. If the interest is for the use of money, the return of the principal returns the ownership and use of money to the lender since they cannot be separated. A separate charge for use, which is returned with ownership, is to sell something that does not exist; namely, use apart from ownership.

The real question is whether it is just or equitable to sell nothing, independent of the agreement and consent of the purchaser. Justice, which is the "habit whereby a man renders to each one his due by a constant and perpetual will,"[17] demands equality in exchange. On a practical level, this means that to act justly, there must be an equality between things exchanged. Nothing is equivalent only with nothing, and therefore no price can be assigned to it. To charge a price for nothing is evidently unjust because the two sides are unequal.

Commenting on the alternative description, selling the same thing twice, Walter Farrell, in his commentary on Aquinas, summarises: "It is absurdly simple to understand that to charge a man twice for the same thing is always unjust; yet that is precisely what usury does, it sells the same thing twice. The trick is possible only when the thing sold or loaned is consumed in its very first use, things like

---

[16] Aquinas, *On Evil*, q13, a4.
[17] Aquinas, *Summa Theologiae: Secunda Secundae*, 1–91, q58, a1.

wine or sandwiches or money. When we demand, over and above the return of the original sum of money loaned [in a *mutuum*], an added amount for the use of the money, our act is the same as selling a man a glass of wine and then charging him for the privilege of drinking it."[18]

In summary, Aquinas's argument against usury rests on the distinction between ownership and use in things. With regard to money, the substance of money is its use. Once used, it is no longer the property of the borrower. To treat the use of such a thing as something that can be separated from ownership and to charge for it, is to charge for something that does not exist. This is against justice by defrauding the borrower and stealing from him.[19]

One might ask, if one cannot charge interest to profit from a *mutuum* loan, why would one ever extend credit to someone in this way? In short, charity can be the only motivator, since to make any profit over and above the principal is against justice. The sole motivator could only be the desire to help a friend (however distant) in need.

1.2.3 Personal guarantees

To conclude the discussion of Aquinas's argument, there is one last concept to explore that has the benefit of rendering what is a difficult topic more accessible. St. Francis Xavier (1502–1556), in a letter to a fellow priest on hearing confessions, talking specifically of usury, recommends a line of questioning: "What is the system that they follow in barter, in loans, and in the whole matter of *security for contracts?*"[20] In following this advice, there is to be found a heuristic which makes identifying usury today simple while maintaining all the substance of the Scholastic position.

Security on a contract consists of some specified set

---

[18] Walter Farrell, *A Companion of the Summa*, 3rd ed. (New York: Sheed and Ward, 1940), 239.
[19] Odd Langholm, *The Aristotelian Analysis of Usury* (Bergen: Universitetsforlaget, 1984), 144.
[20] Henry James Coleridge, *The Life and Letters of St. Francis Xavier*, vol. II (London: Burns and Oates, 1872), 118.

of assets which are pledged as collateral in a contract and which guarantee that the contracting parties fulfil their obligations.[21] The easiest way to identify what is acting as security in a contract is to consider what happens when things go wrong. Consider a mortgage in which the borrower defaults. The mortgage provider has recourse to the house to make good the balance of the mortgage. That is to say that the bank can repossess the house and sell it to cover its losses. The mortgage contract stipulates that the house is the security on the loan, i.e., the thing that guarantees that the loan is ultimately repaid. Of course, it could be the case that the house was bought when prices were high and the borrower defaults when prices are low, so that foreclosure (repossession and sale of the house by the lender) does not cover the mortgage balance. If the contract states that the house is the only security in the agreement, this is a risk which the lender faces, who would have no recourse in law to further action against the defaulting borrower.[22]

Applying this same analysis to a *mutuum* contract, what acts as the security when things go wrong and the borrower defaults? In this circumstance, since the loaned goods have been consumed (in the case of money, used, meaning the borrower no longer has any legal title to it), the specific loaned goods cannot be the property acting as security. The thing that acts as security is only the personal promise of the borrower to repay the *mutuum* loan. Justinian's description of a *mutuum* states that the lender transfers ownership of their property "on condition that the receiver shall transfer

---

[21] Cf. Dickson, *Usury: Frequently Asked Questions*.
[22] This is an oversimplification of mortgage terms for the sake of argument. "In all European countries, mortgages are recourse loans. When the market value of a borrower's house upon foreclosure does not cover the mortgage debt, the lender can claim the borrower's personal (unsecured) assets, as well as their future income. In contrast, many U. S. states are non-recourse." Alin Marius Andries et al., "Recourse and (Strategic) Mortgage Defaults: Evidence from Changes in Housing Market Laws," *DNB Working Paper*, DeNederlandscheBank, no. 727 (October 2021): 2.

to us, ... other things of the same kind and quality."[23] This promise, the personal guarantee, creates a personal liability for the borrower which gives the lender recourse to the borrower and the borrower's assets to recoup anything owed. Note that this is categorically different from a loan (of any sort) with named, physical security. In cases with a personal guarantee, the borrower can be pursued for any and all of his wealth, until the loan is repaid. In cases without a personal guarantee, the contracts terminate in some specific asset, the security. Once neither party has title to that security, all rights under the contract come to an end.

It is this which distinguishes *mutuum* lending from any other type of lending. The borrower in the former gives a promise of repayment. In the latter, the borrower specifies some assets which act as the backstop to the contract. This idea will be developed in more depth as other contracts are considered.

1.3 THE FIXED VALUE OF FUNGIBLES

So far, the assertion of Roman Law has been assumed, that the measure of equality in a *mutuum* is the kind and quantity of goods. It has been established that the things whose ownership is transferred in a *mutuum* are fungible, returned in kind and not returned in particular. What remains to be verified is how the equivalence of such goods is to be determined. This is important because to fulfil his obligations under a *mutuum*, the borrower must repay the debt. If repayment consists in something that includes interest as a matter of justice (to maintain an equality), then Aquinas's argument will have missed an important point. For example, is the equivalence of two bottles of wine determined by their quantity, type, and year, or is the equivalence determined by the enjoyment to the drinker? The latter may make the repayment smaller or larger than the loan. Is the equivalence of a sum of money based in its quantity or in its value? Again, the

---

[23] Justinian, *The Institutes of Justinian*, 130.

latter may be subject to other factors besides quantity.

To find an answer to this, we must look more closely at fungible goods, and to our aid comes the so-called Andrean argument, named after Joannes Andreae (1270–1348), about the value of fungibles. Goods capable of being loaned in a *mutuum*, he argues, have an equivalence fixed by their number.

> Things fixed in number, weight, or measure have an intrinsic value set upon them by their determined quantity; when the lender of such goods expects to receive a greater quantity than he gave, he attempts to make his goods "worth more than their nature"; consequently, he acts unjustly and unnaturally.[24]

Consider a *mutuum* loan of six bottles of wine to be repaid a month later. In arguing that the bottles have a value set on them by their determined quantity, Andreae is claiming that the measure of that value is intrinsic, rather that extrinsic. This means that the value to be returned is measured by their quantity (of the same type and year, etc.), not by the relative pleasure or enjoyment afforded or any other such extrinsic measure. This is further made clear by claiming that receiving a greater quantity would be to make the goods worth *more than their nature* which, by definition, must concern an intrinsic measure rather an extrinsic measure. If in justice the *mutuum* loan of wine requires equality in giving and receiving, one uses an extrinsic measure in asserting the equality of seven bottles in return for six.

The argument makes the case that the only objective basis for establishing an equality between fungible goods is the measure inherent to the thing itself. The measure is, in a sense, built in. Wheat is measured in bushels, wine in bottles, money in number. To hold that there is an equality

---

[24] Andreae, VI, *De Regulis iuris*, "Peccatum," 12, cited in Noonan, *The Scholastic Analysis of Usury*, 66.

between ten and eleven units of any of these goods *solely on the basis of the goods themselves* has no rational basis. With money therefore, it is the numerical quantity which determines equivalence for equitable giving and receiving. Treating two different sums as the same (the principal as the same as the principal plus interest) and demanding that the greater be repaid is unjust.

To avoid equivocation and confusion, one must distinguish this means of establishing equality in a *mutuum* from the general question of pricing in a marketplace.

In economic terms, there are two things which are used to explain the price of a commodity:[25] the relative scarcity or plenty, and the utility for the owner that "can be expressed as a single principle, marginal utility."[26] These two things, in tandem with supply and demand, contribute to the establishing of general prices in a market.[27] Human utility in this twofold analysis is subjective and conditioned by the will of the potential or actual owner. Money is a medium of exchange and fulfils its function by equating different things through a price measure. Indeed, equality of a thing with money, its price, varies with conditions. Therefore, there can be no question of establishing precisely the objective price of a bottle of wine or a house or any other such commodity, either fungible and non-fungible, when using money as the measure, and the only way to do it sensitively is through the market.[28]

---

[25] The question of price can be evaluated without entering into the more fundamental question of whether money itself is a commodity which is vendible at a price. The question at present is the extent to which there is any basis to charge for money in a *mutuum*.
[26] John D. Mueller, *Redeeming Economics: Rediscovering the Missing Element* (Wilmington, DE: ISI Books, 2014), 60.
[27] This is merely to restate the economic argument in short, not to suggest its perfection and convenience in practice.
[28] Note that arguments to the effect that usury is a corollary of the medieval theory of just price — a theory which is said to establish precisely the objective price of goods — are simply false. Cf. Raymond de Roover, "The Concept of the Just Price: Theory and Economic Policy," *The Journal of Economic History* 18, no. 4 (1958): 418–34.

A unique situation arises with money when considering its price because it is both the measure and the thing to be measured. Is it possible to assert that the price of money is different from its nominal value? Andreae argues in the negative, since the intrinsic measure is the only basis. Indeed, Aquinas, commenting on Aristotle's comparison of money to other goods, states that "all other things have a certain utility from themselves, whereas money does not, but is only a measure of the utility of other things."[29] That is to say, money is a way of quantifying and comparing the utility, for man, of all the goods and services available in a market. This is the reason why Aquinas asserts: "To take more money for something less appears to be nothing more than to change the measure in receiving and giving, which manifestly contains a lack of equity."[30] If money is both the measure, and measured, and in being measured can be equal to non-identical nominal values (i.e., £100 is equivalent to £120) then one distorts the measure in the very act of using it. As Bernadine of Sienna argues: "Precision in the calculation of value does not exist in nature except in things whose value is conceived in terms of number, weight, or measure."[31] Andreae's argument is that it is possible to be precise in determining an equality of money (or any good) loaned in a *mutuum*.

A *mutuum* contract treats goods as fungible, and while there are extrinsic means of pricing goods, this is not an objective basis for establishing equity in a *mutuum*. Fungible goods have an inherent and objective measure, and therefore this measure must be used to satisfy justice. There is no price of money in a *mutuum* apart from the quantity loaned.

---

[29] Thomas Aquinas, *Commentary on the Sentences, Book III, Distinctions 23–60*, trans. Chris Decaen and Beth Mortensen (forthcoming from The Aquinas Institute for the Study of Sacred Doctrine), d37, a6, "Whether Usury is a Sin."
[30] Aquinas, *Sent.* III, d37, a6, "Whether Usury is a Sin."
[31] Armstrong, *The Idea of a Moral Economy*, 65.

1.4 EXTRINSIC TITLES: THE CASE FOR DAMAGES

No discussion of usury is complete without the concept of extrinsic titles, which gives the lender the right to make charges over and above the principal. An extrinsic title permits a particular charge in excess of the principal for something outside the contract rather than something intrinsic to the contract itself. These were described by Benedict XIV in *Vix Pervenit* in 1745 when he wrote: "at times together with the loan contract, certain other titles—which are not at all intrinsic to the contract—may run parallel with it. From these other titles, entirely just and legitimate reasons arise to demand something over and above the amount due on the contract."[32]

These titles are called extrinsic because they are not essential to a *mutuum*, but are associated with a particular *mutuum* loan due to the circumstances surrounding the transaction. This is the context in which the word "interest" first arises, taking its name from the Latin *intersum esse*, signifying "the licit difference between the principal and repayment of the loan."[33] Usury analysis prior to the development of extrinsic titles called *anything* taken above the principal usury. The use of the term "interest" is slightly misleading here. It would be best to call it damages, to reflect the substance of the historical discussion and to avoid equivocation with interest as usury.

Extrinsic titles fall under three headers: *poena detentori* (penalty for late payment); *damnum emergens* (emergent loss); and *lucrum cessans* (gain ceasing). The first covers damages suffered after the loan comes to term, the latter two are titles to damages suffered during the term of the loan.

---

[32] Benedict XIV, *Vix Pervenit*, par. 9.
[33] John H. Munro, "The Medieval Origins of the Financial Revolution: Usury, *Rentes*, and Negotiability," *The International History Review* 25, no. 3 (2003): 551. Alternately rendered as *id quod* interest: see Patrick Cleary, *The Church and Usury: An Essay on Some Historical and Theological Aspects of Money Lending* (first published in 1972; reprinted Hawthorne, CA: Christian Book Club of America, 1984), 91.

Poena detentori can be thought of as "penalty for tardy payment either awarded by a court of law (*judicialis*) or stipulated by contract in advance (*conventionalis*)."[34] If the borrower is unable to pay the lender back at the time agreed in the contract, and the lender suffers some real loss on account of not having the money when expected, the borrower is justifiably held to have caused a damage to the lender which can be charged for. If, however, the loan was set on such short terms that the lender and borrower intended late payment as a condition of the loan, this would be *in fraudem usura*, that is, merely a contractual fiction to hide usury. *Poena detentori* presents no challenge to the usury position, and allows some non-profitable increment on a *mutuum*.

Damnum emergens is a title covering cases of loss arising for the lender surrounding the loan. The earliest example of this principle in action is found in the Franciscan *Montes Pietatis*. These charitable lending houses developed in the fifteenth century to lend money to the poor, offering an alternative to those suffering from the difficulties of indebtedness to usurers.[35] Despite controversy, it became settled opinion that the *Montes* could charge fees on loans to defray the expenses of administering the loans. The cost to the *Montes* incurred through wages, administration, etc., were real losses with respect to the loans. Note, however, that the intention behind lending with the *Montes* was the charitable relief of the poor, and not the running of a profit-making enterprise.[36]

The third title, *lucrum cessans*, can be distinguished from "emergent loss ... by the fact that emergent loss causes detriment to goods possessed; but *lucrum cessans* causes *a loss of goods which you expect to possess but do not*."[37]

---

[34] de Roover, *San Bernardino of Siena and Saint Antonino of Florence*, 31.

[35] A concise and useful history is given by Anscar Parsons, "Economic Significance of the 'Montes Pietatis,'" *Franciscan Studies* 1, no. 3 (1941): 3–28.

[36] Cf. Noonan, *The Scholastic Analysis of Usury*, 295; Dempsey, *Interest and Usury*, 179.

[37] Dempsey, *Interest and Usury*, 171 (emphasis added), also citing Juan de Lugo, *De Justicia et Jure*, 25:70.

This third title is of special interest because the argument that the usury prohibition is no longer applicable, or even relevant, often runs along the following lines: (1) the medieval and late-medieval economy was one in which there was very little opportunity for profitable investment to be made;[38] (2) the extrinsic title of *lucrum cessans*, in particular, introduced the concept of legitimately charging something over and above the principal in a *mutuum* where an alternative profitable opportunity had been lost on account of the loan; (3) in the modern and early modern economy, there is never a shortage of opportunities to put money to use to produce a surplus; (4) therefore, interest on a loan is not usury in the modern economy, but *lucrum cessans*. As is plain, if this were true, it would remove any practical significance from the arguments outlined thus far.[39] It is necessary therefore to look deeper and identify the circumstances under which *lucrum cessans* may be claimed.

A summary of the various positions on *lucrum cessans* helps us to see the terms and range of the debate (c. 1300–c. 1700). Aquinas's argument, which Scotus also makes, is that one "must not sell that which he has not yet and may be prevented in many ways from having."[40] Conrad Summenhart (1450–1502) opposes this view on the basis that money is the tool of the merchant, and just as one would be obliged to compensate a workman for depriving him of the use of his tools for a

---

[38] Noonan, *The Scholastic Analysis of Usury*, 249: "This increase in commerce rendered it objectively more probable that a lender underwent a true loss of profit when he loaned his money instead of using it in business." Parsons, "Economic Significance of the 'Montes Pietatis,'" 25: "In the Middle Ages this extrinsic title [*lucrum cessans*] was normally lacking, whereas it is normally present today." Dempsey, *Interest and Usury*, 177: "Lugo, on the other hand, furnishes many parenthetical remarks by which he indicates that he believes that the presence of facts upon which titles are based is very general indeed"—this last quotation showing that the argument is not merely recent.

[39] Cf. Paul S. Mills, "Interest in Interest: The Old Testament Ban on Interest and Its Implications for Today," Doctoral Thesis, Cambridge University, 1989. Mills argues that the general admission of *lucrum cessans* was the beginning of the end of the usury prohibition.

[40] Aquinas, *Summa Theologiae: Secunda Secundae*, 1–91, q78, a2, ad1.

period of time, so too one must compensate the merchant for depriving him of the tools of his trade. Summenhart, in one of a number of conditions he requires to charge *lucrum cessans*,[41] stipulates that "the title [not] be used ... where one is bound by a precept of charity."[42] Since charity is the sole motivator for *mutuum* loans, this seems to undermine his own argument. Cajetan defends Aquinas's position from the attacks of Summenhart. While recognising that money has a peculiar power for the merchant, Cajetan distinguishes between the "power [of money] insofar as it is simply an exchange medium"[43] and "not absolutely, but insofar as it is subject to the industry of such a businessman."[44] He argues that the latter power is not common to all money, contra Summenhart, and that a merchant's money is reduced from the latter to the former state voluntarily, when a merchant loans in a *mutuum*.

Domingo de Soto (1494–1560) qualifies Cajetan's argument on the power of money, but more critically argues against the requirement for charitable intent. This is expanded by Navarrus's argument that intention is not the measure of equality in a loan, but justice and "the equality of things."[45] Furthermore, he replies to Summenhart's argument that being deprived of the tools of one's trade has a pecuniary estimation that can be sought for its own sake in a loan. Lessius extends this, countering Cajetan and arguing that, "the loan ... is the mediate cause of the loss of business profit to him [the lender]. Therefore, the lender can charge for having reduced money from a fecund to a sterile state."[46] The mere fact that money is loaned in a *mutuum* by a merchant is sufficient title to claim *lucrum cessans*. Again, intent is not a relevant consideration in this analysis, and the arguments have developed to such an extent from

---

[41] Noonan, *The Scholastic Analysis of Usury*, 251.
[42] Noonan, 251.
[43] Cajetan, *Commentarium in summam theologicam S. Thomae Aquinatis*, Leon. edition (Rome, 1882), II-II, q78, a2, III, cited in Noonan, 253.
[44] Ibid.
[45] Noonan, 260.
[46] Noonan, 262.

Summenhart to Lessius that in general there are arguments in favour of *lucrum cessans* on the majority of loans. What was usury under early analysis would, through these arguments, be permitted under another name as *lucrum cessans*.

Now, further consideration of *lucrum cessans* as a charge for "loss of goods which you expect to possess but do not" (i.e., loss of future gain) begs the following strange-sounding question. In what sense can it be said that one has future profit now? Only in the sense that one has taken the necessary action to bring about the course of events that would yield that profit, but not in the sense of actually owning and possessing something in the future. The future has not happened, so you cannot own anything in it right now; you can only own real things. But if you don't actually possess the future profit yet, you can't lose it, because to lose something you must first have it in the relevant sense for it to be lost.

Future contingents, the subject matter of *lucrum cessans*, or "opportunity costs" to use a contemporary name, are not real assets that you can rent, sell, alienate, lease, or do any other such thing with. To charge someone for something that doesn't exist, that merely exists hypothetically, is to charge for nothing. This is precisely the injustice which is the object of Aquinas's argument against usury. "He must not sell that which he has not yet and may be prevented in many ways from having."[47]

Moreover, excepting cases of forcible loans by city-states or their modern equivalents, the lender is always free to loan or not loan. Integral to this voluntary action is the exclusion of other courses of action that could be pursued with that money. This exclusion of all other courses of action is inseparable from the choice. One cannot both chop down an apple tree to use the wood to make furniture and expect to harvest apples from the tree in future years. If the owner chooses to fell the tree, it would be absurd for him to demand from the stump, or from nature, compensation for the future apples that he *could* have had from that tree

---

[47] Aquinas, *Summa Theologiae: Secunda Secundae*, 1–91, q78, a2, ad1.

but now cannot. Choosing one course of action *de facto* means the others are merely consequences in the mind, not actually existing things. It only becomes possible to make this claim for interest on account of opportunity cost in a *mutuum* because it is agreed between people. It is possible for a person to return the principal plus interest in a way that it is not possible for a felled tree to return apples. It is precisely because the agreements are made between people that care should be taken to ensure that justice is satisfied.

Of the three overarching titles to damages, then, *poena detentori*, arising from loss after the term of a loan, is based in some real existing loss for which compensation can be actually charged. Of two titles that run during the term of the *mutuum* loan itself, *damnum emergens* has a basis in some actually existing property or loss of property which can be quantified and, on the whole, the lender has a real claim to compensation from the borrower for such eventualities. *Lucrum cessans*, the most contentious, and the most fatal in its historical development for the usury doctrine, is however grounded in hypotheticals. To charge for non-existent things is unjust. Hypothetical future scenarios do not exist as property in any relevant sense that can give rise to rents or charges.

A historical point brings the discussion of extrinsic titles to a close. Justifications of *mutuum* lending for profit as a trade in and of itself are rarely defended from Aquinas to the sixteenth century (the first argument of this kind by Salmasius will be discussed below). While *lucrum cessans* was a controversial title that gained ground and appears to legitimise such business on different grounds, it must be taken in tandem with the motivating factor for such loans, namely charity. Therefore, even if one were to admit *lucrum cessans* as a legitimate title, since credit card lending, student loans, and consumer finance (buy now, pay later with non-zero interest) businesses exist *in order* to profit from *mutuum* lending via interest, the conditions for charging *lucrum cessans* are not met and therefore the charges are unjustified.

1.5 TWO OTHER ARGUMENTS AGAINST USURY

Before proceeding to address the objections raised against the case thus made, it will be instructive to look at two particular arguments that have been made against usury. These are the Aristotelian *barren metal argument*, and Hilaire Belloc's *production-consumption* argument. In contrast to how the argument has proceeded thus far, considering how the nature of one contract differs from another, both these arguments focus on one aspect of loan contracts at the expense of others.

With regard to the *barren metal* argument, there are two viewpoints which emerge from the history of the debate about money, aptly summarised by Noonan: "Money is always sterile if taken by itself, and it is always fertile if it is identified with what it buys."[48] It appears as though one can describe the one thing, money, in two contrary ways. The first group claims that money is merely barren metal which does not produce any increase. The second theory is that money is fertile and increases.

Centuries before the integration of Roman legal principles into the usury debate, Aristotle had explicitly considered the question of usury in his political philosophy. He argues that: "usury is most reasonably hated, because its gain comes from money itself and not from that for the sake of which money was invented."[49] His argument runs that money is a barren thing and does not give birth (literally: τόκος) to itself. To charge for the use of money is to treat it as something contrary to its nature. Since it is unnatural, it cannot be chosen as a course of action. Indeed, of all forms of accumulating wealth, it is "most contrary to nature."[50]

Joseph Schumpeter (1883–1950), professor of economic history at Harvard and author of the introduction to

---

[48] Noonan, *The Scholastic Analysis of Usury*, 395.
[49] Aristotle, *Politics*, trans. H. Rackham, Loeb Classical Library vol. 21 (Cambridge, MA: Harvard University Press, 1944), 1258b1.
[50] Aristotle, *Politics*, 1258b1.

Dempsey's book on usury, occupies the extreme opposite position. He argues that "saving and investment must be interpreted to mean saving of some real factors of production and their conversion into real capital goods, such as buildings, machines, raw materials; and, though 'in the form of money,' it is these physical capital goods that are 'really' lent when an industrial borrower arranges for a loan."[51] That is to say, since capital goods can be used to generate an increase over time, and money can be treated as transparent or stand in for the goods themselves, it is not sterile but fruitful. Since these real capital goods are "really" lent in a loan, and themselves give rise to profit, it is erroneous to claim that one cannot charge interest because money is sterile.

How are such differences to be reconciled? These opposing viewpoints rest on the very fact that money is by design a measure of things. As to the physical object of money, clearly of itself it neither multiplies nor provides any increment when left, as John Calvin (1509–1564) describes it, *in sacculo*, in a bag.[52] When considered in light of its specific and primary purpose, that is, as a means of exchange, it does take on the characteristic described by Schumpeter. It is valuable because it can be converted into real goods through exchange. Therefore, it is convenient to think that a loan (*mutuum* or any other kind) of money is a means of acquiring other goods.

Now both ways of describing money are unproblematic considered on their own. The nature of money and the extent to which it can be thought of as either transparent (convertible with goods for which it can be exchanged) or opaque (merely a physical object) runs throughout the debate. In times when money was entirely physical, unlike

---

[51] Joseph Alois Schumpeter, *The History of Economic Analysis* ([n.p.]: [n.pub.], 1943), 265.

[52] It is clear that Calvin's mention of the topic in passing does not represent a considered perspective; yet, due to his enormous influence in Protestant countries, his writing had a disproportionate effect in accelerating the general acceptance of usury.

the present day, the lived reality of handling gold and precious metals for exchange provided the tangible backdrop to this argument. In a contemporary setting, this historical perspective is often lost and, therefore, the argument less visceral. However, noting where each interpretation is used in arguments is a useful tool to isolate the premises and establish the veracity of a position.

Invoking a *production-consumption* distinction,[53] Belloc defines usury in two ways: "Usury has nothing to do with the taking of high or low interest, ... usury is the taking of any interest whatever upon an unproductive loan."[54] He also writes, "Usury, then, is essentially a claim to increment, or extra wealth, which is not there to be claimed."[55] Belloc's fundamental concern, situated within the context of the sheer size of war loans and the interest accruing on them, was the creation of real wealth. In contributing money to a productive project and claiming interest, Belloc justifies interest on account of the return of the enterprise. In a loan for the purposes of consumption, that is, to buy a house or food and the like, there is no profit generated by the activity since the money is simply consumed. Indeed, for Belloc, usury "is a practice which diminishes the capital wealth of the needy and eats it up to the profit of the lender."[56]

Given the arguments outlined in this work so far, one can see why Edward Coyne (1896–1958), an Irish Jesuit and contemporary of Belloc, could argue against this

---

[53] Belloc's *production-consumption* distinction is important to consider, as it continues to play a role in contemporary debate: see Brian M. McCall, *The Church and the Usurers: Unprofitable Lending for the Modern Economy* ([n.p.]: Sapientia Press of Ave Maria University, 2013); Anthony M. Fernandez, Levi A. Russell, and Anthony M. Gentile, "Usury and Interest: Correcting Modern Errors," Leonine Institute for Catholic Social Teaching, 22 July 2020, https://leoinstitute.org/policy-papers/.
[54] Hilaire Belloc, *Economics for Helen* ([n.p.]: St. George Educational Trust, 1999), 112.
[55] Belloc, 115.
[56] Belloc, 115.

production-consumption distinction. "The productivity or the unproductivity of the loan does not enter at all into the essence of usury."[57] The essential distinction which makes interest on a loan of money usurious is the manner in which the goods are treated by the contract. A *mutuum* transfers ownership of the goods from the lender to the borrower. A *mutuum* also treats the goods as fungible and to be returned in kind. Therefore, any interest in such an agreement is a charge for nothing (the use of the thing separate from ownership). Belloc's argument is incomplete because the use to which the fungible goods are put is only a secondary consideration to the analysis seen so far. This view is strengthened from the point of view of economic history by Odd Langholm (b. 1928), who argues: "The impression given by a systematic study of the Scholastic treatises on usury does not confirm the notion that they mainly envisaged such loans [i.e., production loans]."[58]

In summary, usury can occur only in a *mutuum* which governs the transfer of ownership of goods treated as fungible. Ownership and use are indistinguishable in this class of goods. Therefore, there can be no use, separate from ownership, that gives rise to a charge. Since the money is repaid in full by returning the same quantity as was lent, the debt is discharged and there are consequently no grounds for any charge in the form of interest. To attempt such a charge would be to sell something non-existent. It would be to sell use separate from ownership when they are, in fact, inseparable. This is unjust.

Extrinsic titles provide grounds to charge for damages which are real losses that the lender incurs in extending a *mutuum* loan to a borrower. Of these the most contentious and fatal historically to the practical prohibition of usury was *lucrum cessans*, the idea of opportunity cost or lost

---

[57] Edward J. Coyne, "Mr. Belloc on Usury," *Studies: An Irish Quarterly Review* 21, no. 82 (1932): 289.
[58] Langholm, *The Aristotelian Analysis of Usury*, 135.

profit. This concept does not entail the sale of anything real in the sense that it can be rented or charged for and, therefore, *lucrum cessans* is not a legitimate extrinsic title.

Finally, the idea of *barren metal* is a poetic expression of an argument against an injustice which was well known even in ancient times. Belloc's *production-consumption* approach is incomplete because the use to which the goods loaned in a *mutuum* are put, productive or consumptive, is not an essential part of the contract itself—but it partially reflects the fact that fungible goods which are the object of *mutua* are *de facto* consumed in their use.

2
CAN INTEREST BE CHARGED FOR OTHER THINGS BESIDES THE USE OF MONEY?

THE argument outlined above demonstrates why usury is a charge for nothing and that this is unjust. It does not take long, however, to find the economists' position that: "the doctrine [of usury] has been buried long ago by both classical and modern economists."[1] Is this really the case, or is this merely the case in practice while the principled arguments against usury remain sound? The volume of discussion to draw from is vast. It includes what has been covered so far (c. 1250–c. 1700), continues from the end of the Middle Ages through the birth of classical economics with the publication of Adam Smith's *The Wealth of Nations* in 1776 and on up to the present day. For present purposes, it is sufficient to discuss the most biting arguments to see whether there are good reasons to accept a charge for something other than use or extrinsic titles. This can be done in three groups.

The first are arguments grounded in a *mutuum*. These arose during the close of the Middle Ages, when Scholasticism was still a collective intellectual endeavour. The second are transitional arguments, which can be derived from the argument between Adam Smith and Jeremy Bentham about usury. The third is an analysis of the economic arguments in favour of interest to understand whether they really do bury the idea of usury.

---

[1] Edwin Cannan et al., "Saving and Usury: A Symposium," *The Economic Journal* 42, no. 165 (1932): 131. In the words of Eugen von Böhm-Bawerk: "As regards the development of the theoretical interest problem, the whole period, notwithstanding its length, and notwithstanding the great number of writers who flourished during it, is rather barren. Men were fighting, as we shall see, not for the centre of the problem, but for an outpost of it which, from a theoretical standpoint, was of comparatively subordinate importance." *Capital and Interest: A Critical History of Economic Theory* (London; New York: Macmillan and Co., 1890), 14.

The breadth of economic thinkers makes it challenging to identify a sufficiently narrow field with which to engage.[2] John Maynard Keynes (1883–1946) provides a notable, albeit qualified, exception amongst the ranks of economists whose thought has shaped recent history. In his most influential work, first published in 1936, he states:

> There remains an allied, but distinct, matter where for centuries, indeed for several millenniums, enlightened opinion held for certain and obvious a doctrine which the classical school has repudiated as childish, but which deserves rehabilitation and honour.... I was brought up to believe that the attitude of the Medieval Church to the rate of interest was inherently absurd, and that the subtle discussions aimed at distinguishing the return on money-loans from the return to active investment were merely jesuitical attempts to find a practical escape from a foolish theory. But I now read these discussions as the honest intellectual effort to keep separate what the classical theory has inextricably confused together.[3]

While there is much that can be said about this view,[4] Keynes had earlier in his career already expressed a position

---

[2] Bernard Dempsey (1903–1960) engaged with Fisher, Böhm-Bawerk, Hayek, Keynes, Wicksell, and Menger, among others, in his work *Interest and Usury*; economic historians such as W. J. Ashley, *An Introduction to English Economic History and Theory: The End of the Middle Ages*, part 2 (London: Longmans, Green & Co., 1894); Robert S. Lopez, *The Commercial Revolution of the Middle Ages, 950–1350* (Cambridge: Cambridge University Press, 1977); Karl Polanyi, *The Great Transformation: The Political and Economic Origins of Our Times* (Boston, MA: Beacon Press, 2001); Schumpeter, *The History of Economic Analysis*; R. H. Tawney, *Religion and the Rise of Capitalism: A Historical Study* (Drayton, Middlesex: Penguin Books, 1937) are good reference points for their overall analysis of the topic.
[3] John Maynard Keynes, *The General Theory of Employment, Interest and Money* (Hertfordshire: Wordsworth Editions Ltd., 2017), 304.
[4] M. G. Hayes, "Keynes's Liquidity Preference and the Usury Doctrine: Their Connection and Continuing Policy Relevance," *Review of Social Economy* 75, no. 4 (2017): 400–416.

common to economists about the relationship between economic analysis and morality:

> I see us free, therefore, to return to some of the most sure and certain principles of religion and traditional virtue — that avarice is a vice, that the exaction of usury is a misdemeanour, and the love of money is detestable, that those walk most truly in the paths of virtue and sane wisdom who take least thought for the morrow.... But beware! The time for all this is not yet. For at least another hundred years we must pretend to ourselves and to every one that fair is foul and foul is fair; for foul is useful and fair is not. Avarice and usury and precaution must be our gods for a little longer still. For only they can lead us out of the tunnel of economic necessity into daylight.[5]

This rather dismal perspective points to the choice of antagonists in this analysis. The Austrian school takes this perspective — the subordination of moral questions to merely economic analysis — and follows it to its logical conclusion. In its libertarian aspect, the Austrian school places special emphasis and priority on the independence of the free market in determining economic outcomes. This is so fundamental a position in their line of thought that from it usury can be defended outright as a social blessing.[6] There is also a clear line of Austrian economists in which to identify consistent strands of thought,[7] itself anchored in the analysis of the French economist Jacques Turgot

---

[5] John Maynard Keynes, *Essays in Persuasion* (New York: W. W. Norton & Co., 1963), 358–73.

[6] Glen Tenney, "The Social Blessings of 'Usury,'" *Mises Daily Articles* (blog), accessed 3 July 2021, https://mises.org/library/social-blessings-usury; Alyssa Labat and Walter Block, "Money Does Not Grow on Trees: An Argument for Usury," *Journal of Business Ethics* 106, no. 3 (2012): 383–87.

[7] Carl Menger (1840–1921) taught Eugen von Böhm-Bawerk (1851–1914) who in turn taught Ludwig von Mises (1881–1973). Von Mises taught both Friedrich Hayek (1899–1992) and Murray Rothbard (1926–1995). The latter taught Walter Block (1941–present).

(1727–1781) who is credited with developing the concept of time-preference.[8]

These economists' approach can best be summed up by the Austrian economist Böhm-Bawerk: "The problem of loan interest is pursued [during the Middle-Ages] till it falls in with the general problem of interest."[9] That is to say, in economics, modern interest is considered first as a general economic phenomenon and only then applied to the different aspects of the economy. This stands in contrast to the medieval approach of primarily analysing particular facets of individual economic action, contracts being one aspect, and only secondarily deriving general economic principles.[10]

2.1 COUNTERARGUMENTS ROOTED IN A *MUTUUM*

Two main early counterarguments to Aquinas's argument are relevant. The first distinguishes "lack of use" as something with a pecuniary estimation; the second separates the value of money from ownership.

Regarding the first, Conrad Summenhart in his work *De Contractibus* makes a novel counter to Aquinas's argument, claiming that it "misses the point."[11] Although it found little

---

[8] "Seldom can there have been a more grateful task than was the refutation of this doctrine in the second half of the eighteenth century. Long ago smitten with internal decay — detested by some, despised by others — forced to lean on very pitiful scientific props — it had long outlived its life, and only raised its head in the present like some old ruin. The task was taken up by Turgot, and performed with ability as remarkable as its results were brilliant." Böhm-Bawerk, *Capital and Interest: A Critical History of Economic Theory*, 54.

[9] Böhm-Bawerk, *Capital and Interest*, 59.

[10] "If we seek to locate the purpose of Scholastic economic ethics in the macro-economy, then we are on the wrong track." Langholm, *The Aristotelian Analysis of Usury*, 148. This opens up the more fundamental question of the change in moral footing of the debate between the medieval and modern periods. On this change, see especially Mueller, *Redeeming Economics: Rediscovering the Missing Element*; Mary L. Hirschfeld, *Aquinas and the Market: Toward a Humane Economy* (Cambridge, MA: Harvard University Press, 2018); Edward Hadas, *Human Goods, Economic Evils: A Moral Approach to the Dismal Science* (Wilmington, DE: ISI Books, 2007); John C. Medaille, *Toward a Truly Free Market* (Newburyport: Intercollegiate Studies Institute, 2014).

[11] Noonan, *The Scholastic Analysis of Usury*, 341.

general acceptance for a hundred years, Noonan asserts that this marked the abandonment of Scholastic usury theory.[12]

For Aquinas, the substance of fungibles consists in their use and, therefore, ownership and use cannot be separated. To charge for use distinct from ownership in a *mutuum* is to charge for something that does not exist, which is contrary to justice. Summenhart argues that what is really going on is not that the lender is charging for the use of money separate from its ownership, but rather that he is charging for *his own lack of use*. The return of the principal at the term of the *mutuum* is not equivalent with that which was lent because the *use during the intervening period* has not been returned. This privation "of a consumptible for a period has a value distinct from the value of the substance of the consumptible"[13] and this privation "has a pecuniary estimation."[14] This same argument is received and promoted by Claude Salmasius (1588–1653) more than a century later.[15]

A privation can be thought of as the lack of a quality of some substance. However, this lack of some quality is not property in the sense that one can exercise the ordinary rights of ownership over it. One cannot alienate one's lack of use to another. What would it mean to buy (or sell) the lack of use of some property outside the discussion of a *mutuum*? Because the lack of use is not property in the relevant sense, it cannot give rise to a charge. If one made an attempt to charge for it, it would be a charge for nothing.

To see this, consider what one pays for in renting a house. If the owner said, the rent is £500 a month, but since I will not be able to use the house for the period you are using it, there is also a charge of £500 for my lack of use, one would quite rightly contest that the lack of use is an essential and inseparable consequence of the fact of rental and cannot be the subject of a separate charge.

---

[12] Noonan, 340–64.
[13] Noonan, 342.
[14] Noonan, 342.
[15] Noonan, 372.

It is telling to note that even Böhm-Bawerk also holds this argument as inconclusive. The discovery of time-preference "relieves him [a follower of Salmasius] of a certain doubtful line of argument that his predecessors were obliged to take... this line of reasoning, always somewhat fatal, was rendered superfluous."[16]

Regarding the second, separating the value of money from ownership, Jacques Turgot (unique for a direct discussion and attempted refutation of Aquinas), in *A Paper on Lending at Interest*, levels an argument against the "distinction often made... between an object hired and consumed during use, and an object which is not consumed during hire."[17] Turgot introduces an extremely novel concept arguing that the borrower may in fact become the owner of the money "considered physically, as a certain quantity of metal. But is he really the owner of the value of the money? Certainly not, since this value is only confided to him for a time, to be repaid on the expiration of the contract."[18] He cannot be accurately described as the owner of the value of the money, since he has to repay it at the term of the contract.

To see the confusion in this statement, it suffices to imagine a friend asking to borrow from you a bottle of wine for his dinner party, promising to give you the equivalent back the following week. In what way could you as the lender make it clear to him that you were indeed giving him ownership of the bottle for a time, but he had no claim on the value of the wine? Since the primary and specific use of money consists in its exchange for other goods of whatever kind, and because of this very action it is a source of value in enabling the owner to accrue to himself goods that he desires, the attempt to distinguish the ownership and value is erroneous as a matter of fact and without basis in any philosophical or metaphysical principles.

---

[16] Böhm-Bawerk, *Capital and Interest*, 50.
[17] Turgot, *The Turgot Collection*, 215.
[18] Turgot, 215.

Again, Böhm-Bawerk is not convinced: "Turgot himself does not hesitate at metaphysical abstraction and legal hairsplitting. To refute the argument that the debtor becomes proprietor of the borrowed money, and that its use consequently belongs to him, he makes out a property in the value of the money, and distinguishes it from the property in the piece of metal."[19] In Turgot's letter, the argument is not developed any further, so it ends up as an ineffective counterargument.

These two counterarguments are grounded directly in a *mutuum* and arise from an ill-formed attempt to distinguish ownership of the properties of a thing from ownership of the thing itself. Properties of things inhere in the things themselves — the money is valuable, the wine is delicious, etc. — and they cannot be owned or transferred independently of the thing itself. Summenhart's and Turgot's attempt to distinguish ownership of properties from ownership of the thing itself has no sound footing.

Although these arguments fail, their merit is that they actually address the arguments laid out against usury in an attempt to justify the practice. The economists' case that follows wholly lacks any distinction of contract, and this begins with the complete repositioning of the debate.

2.2 A TRANSITIONAL DEBATE

The transitional debate can be traced back to Claude Saumaise (Salmasius) (1588–1653). He accordingly receives the gratitude of the Austrian economists Böhm-Bawerk and Rothbard[20] for being the first to defend outright the trade

---

[19] Böhm-Bawerk, *Capital and Interest*, 56.
[20] Böhm-Bawerk (35–36): "The decisive point was reached shortly before the year 1640. As if the barriers of long restraint had all been torn down in one day, a perfect flood of writings broke out in which interest was defended with the utmost vigour, and the flood did not fall till the principle of interest, in the Netherlands at least, had conquered. In this abundant literature, the first place, both in time and rank, was taken by the celebrated Claudius Salmasius... These writings almost by themselves, determined the direction and substance of the theory of interest

of the usurer as just and commendable. He "would rather be called a usurer than a tailor,"[21] a claim that may be uncontroversial today, but was astounding for its audacity at the time.

Salmasius argues that *lucrum cessans* and other extrinsic titles are disguised usury. His arguments are justified with respect to *lucrum cessans*, as per the arguments above — to claim it as a valid extrinsic title is to claim that charging for non-existent things (future contingents) is just. His arguments are less persuasive in the cases of the titles *damnum emergens* and *poena detentori* where these give rise to real costs. Working from this broad set of objections,[22] Salmasius goes on to argue that usury is a business like any other and ought to be encouraged, as the competition between more lenders would depress the rate of interest. This is where Adam Smith (1723–1790) and Jeremy Bentham (1748–1832) enter the discussion, working from the assumption that usury is as sound and permissible a practice as any other.

Bentham's terse roundup of centuries of debate in his *Defence of Usury* is remarkable inasmuch as he limits any understanding of usury to two narrow categories while completely ignoring any medieval discussion on the topic. He claims:

> I know of but two definitions that can possibly be given of usury: one is, the taking of a greater interest than the law allows of: this may be styled the political or legal definition. The other is the taking of a greater interest than it is usual for men to give and take: this may be styled the moral

---

for more than a hundred years, and even in the doctrine of to-day, as we shall see, we may recognise many of their after-effects." Rothbard: "The honor of putting the final boot to the usury prohibition belongs to the seventeenth-century classicist and Dutch Calvinist, Claude Saumaise." Murray N. Rothbard, *An Austrian Perspective on the History of Economic Thought*, vol. 1 (Auburn, AL: Ludwig von Mises Institute, 2006), 144.
[21] Salmasius, *De Usuris*, c. 18, p. 530, cited in Noonan, *The Scholastic Analysis of Usury*, 327.
[22] Salmasius's other objections include the claim that the *census* contract is merely a contractual device invented to conduct usury under another name, a topic that will be addressed below.

one: and this, where the law has not interfered, is plainly enough the only one.[23]

Obviously sympathetic with Salmasius's position, Bentham engaged in a frank argument with Adam Smith on the benefits of establishing a legal maximum to interest rates, independent of any particular contract. Smith's position in favour of interest on loans can be summarised tersely: "As something can everywhere be made by the use of money, something ought everywhere to be paid for the use of it."[24] However, he supported a legal cap on interest. "This rate ought always to be somewhat above the lowest market price, or the price which is commonly paid for the use of money by those who can give the most undoubted security... The legal rate, it is to be observed, though it ought to be somewhat above, ought not to be much above the lowest market rate."[25]

In theoretical matters, Bentham and Smith concur in abandoning the previous understanding and associated opposition to usury.[26] It is telling for the direction of future debate that John Stuart Mill could roundly praise Bentham's writing on usury as the "best extant writing on the subject."[27] It could be said that appreciation for the Scholastic position was, from this point on, a historical observation rather than an animating consideration.

2.3 THE ECONOMIC JUSTIFICATION

This leads directly into the justification for interest from the point of view of economic science. Economists are not concerned with justifying interest against the arguments of

---

[23] Jeremy Bentham, *Defence of Usury* (Gloucester: Dodo Press, 2008), 3.
[24] Smith, *The Wealth of Nations*, 456.
[25] Smith, 457.
[26] Cf. Joseph Persky, "Retrospectives: From Usury to Interest," *The Journal of Economic Perspectives* 21, no. 1 (2007): 227–36.
[27] John Stuart Mill, *Principles of Political Economy: With Some of Their Applications to Social Philosophy* (London: Longmans, Green and Co., 1936), 927.

the Scholastics and, therefore, one does not find arguments beginning "interest on a personally guaranteed loan is not a charge for use, but a charge for x, y, and z." However, select authors are explicit on the rationale for loan interest,[28] and where this occurs, there are three components that compose interest: time preference (also called the time value of money or liquidity preference); a risk premium; and compensation for the effects of inflation.[29]

It is critical to note that this discussion proceeds in light of the distinction above between commodity pricing on the one hand, and establishing the equality of fungibles in a *mutuum* loan on the other. What follows does not deny that the three elements used to explain the value of interest by economists are valid considerations in establishing the prices of commodities, *but only that they do not provide a basis for real charges in a mutuum*. Indeed, for medieval and modern economic thought, "the doctrine of the just price in commodity exchange [commodity pricing] and the doctrine of usury proceed analogously... but the analogy breaks down with the checks and correctives provided by a common estimate."[30] That is to say, the following analysis seeks to make a distinction where Irving Fisher does not. He claims that "the [economic] theory of interest... applies to every species of loan contract."[31] The argument that follows will make the case that the economic theory of interest does not apply to *mutua*, while raising no objections to its application to any other species of loan. For clarity, this is

---

[28] Here the phrase loan interest is used as any economist would use the term: generically, and not specifically with a *mutuum* or other specific contract in mind.
[29] Cf. Gary North, *An Introduction to Christian Economics* (Nutley, NJ: The Craig Press, 1973), 364–66; Alexander Pierre Faure, "Interest Rates 3: Composition of Interest Rates," *SSRN Electronic Journal*, December 23, 2014; David Blake, *Financial Market Analysis* (Chichester: Wiley, 2006), 79–88.
[30] Langholm, *The Aristotelian Analysis of Usury*, 147.
[31] Irving Fisher, *The Theory of Interest: As Determined by Impatience to Spend Income and Opportunity to Invest It* (Mansfield Center, CT: Martino Publishing, 2012), 357.

not an assertion that there is only one economic theory of interest; rather, I assert that all modern economic theories of interest have in common an implicit or explicit justification of interest on a *mutuum*.

2.3.1 Interest as equalising time preference

Firstly, time preference, or the time value of money, is a consequence of valuation of current goods over future goods. What future sum would one need to be promised in order to surrender a current sum? That is, what rate of interest will persuade a lender to lend?

In order to defend the position that time preference gives rise to a real interest charge in a *mutuum*, the syllogism ought to run as follows: People value current goods higher than future goods (major premise). The valuation of goods in such a way gives rise to a real basis for compensation (minor premise). Therefore time-preference is a legitimate title to interest on a loan (conclusion). The problem with this syllogism is the minor premise.

Turgot uses two dimensions to argue for the notion of time preference. The first is that justice must be maintained in an equality between the things exchanged, but this is not to be found in the quantity of the thing, but in the value of the thing to the lender and borrower. "The exchange, being free on both sides, can only be motivated by the preference of each of the contracting parties for the thing he receives over the thing he gives."[32] The second is that it is not merely the weight of metal which needs to be considered to identify an equality, but also the utility at the date of borrowing compared to the date of return. He quotes the proverb "a bird in the hand is worth two in the bush."[33] To this we can add Summenhart's view that "their values arise from their estimation by human prudence."[34] The implication

---

[32] Turgot, *The Turgot Collection*, 213.
[33] Noonan, *The Scholastic Analysis of Usury*, 215.
[34] Noonan, 342; Fisher, *The Theory of Interest*, 96; Langholm, *The Aristotelian Analysis of Usury*, 142.

of this is that in order to establish equality, the quantity of the future good, the return on a loan, must be numerically higher than the current good, the amount loaned.

The fact that current goods can be subjectively valued over future goods is not contended. The principal as one element of an explanation of prices is not questioned here. This fails, however, to provide a reason as to the minor premise, namely the justification of the charge. As already discussed above, there is no means of establishing precisely the objective price of commodity goods; it can be approximated only through the subjective assessment of marginal utility in a market. As such, time preference is a perfectly legitimate means to determine the price of such commodities. Money, or any other such thing loaned in a *mutuum*, has an objective measure inherent to it, and while subjectively it might take on more or less value according to the actor's perspective, this is merely subjective. It does not explain why a subjective preference gives rise to a real charge on a *mutuum*. Böhm-Bawerk attempts to provide a negative justification of the minor premise, arguing that, "for the owner not to realise the higher [subjective] value of his commodity would be an act of unselfishness and charity which could not possibly be translated into a general duty, and as a fact would not be so translated in regard to any other commodity."[35]

However, we have seen that this is precisely the analysis of the Scholastics: because of the demands of justice, the only motivator can be charity. As an economist, however, Böhm-Bawerk is unable to establish any grounds within their science to lay this down as a normative position. With no credible justification of the minor premise specifically as the argument applies to a *mutuum*, the analysis does not justify interest as compensation for time preference in such a loan.

---

[35] Eugen von Böhm-Bawerk, *The Positive Theory of Capital* (New York: G. E. Stechert & Co., 1930), 360.

2.3.2 Risk

Secondly, there is risk, a component of interest covering the fact that

> the lender knows that he may not get his money back. The borrower may go bankrupt, or he may run away with the loan. To compensate the lender for his risk — a factor which can be estimated with some accuracy by modern statistical techniques — he demands a payment above and beyond his time-preference return.[36]

The first positive defence of risk giving rise to a real charge comes from Juan de Medina (1490–1547) in the sixteenth century. "Unsupported by authority, except for the opinions of Summenhart on a somewhat analogous case, Medina has defended a title that no one before him had dared to defend."[37] The argument runs that a lender can justly ask a pledge from his debtor or refuse to lend, and when the borrower cannot provide a pledge of his own property, he can pay another to guarantee the loan, that is, to guarantee the return of the principal (applying the concept of security on a loan as discussed above).

If the borrower can neither provide a pledge nor pay a guarantor, Medina argues that the lender can charge for assuming the risk, in effect making the same charge that the guarantor would have. If one can validly contract between three distinct parties, why should one not be able to enter into the same two contracts with a single counterparty? This is unproblematic in principle, if the lender is really charging for a *real insurance contract*, and in that way mitigating the financial risk in the event of default. However, if the charge is simply for assuming a risk without posting security which could be used to cover costs in the event the potential risks became real risks, then it is just empty verbiage rather than a real action giving rise to a legitimate charge.

---

[36] North, *An Introduction to Christian Economics*, 365.
[37] Noonan, *The Scholastic Analysis of Usury*, 284.

This, however, does seem to beg the question. If risk can be sold, there is no problem; if risk cannot be sold, there is a problem. Commonly speaking, insurance involves a "sale of risk," but this is just common parlance. The facts of insurance bear out the principle that risk is not an asset that one can own, but merely a consequence of the type of thing that one owns. It is a property *of something*. Since it is not something that one can own or can have title to distinct from ownership of an actual thing, it follows that it is not something that one can alienate in a sale. To see this, consider that when one owns a house, the concomitant risks of fire and theft come along with it, but these risks cannot be separated from the underlying thing to which they apply. They can be reduced, certainly, as they are when one ensures that a building is built and equipped according to fire safety regulations, but this only changes the level of risk, and in fact demonstrates that the risk is inseparable from the thing because the risk-reducing actions are taken on the thing itself.

Now, the sale of risk is a shorthand for a pooling of financial assets. An insurer reserves some set of real assets which are converted to cash to cover the cost in the event that a certain set of events happens. In the case of a third-party guarantor on a *mutuum* loan, the guarantor would name some real assets that are the security in case of default.[38] If the lender acts as guarantor, and names some real assets as security, he can justly charge the borrower for this in exactly the same manner as the guarantor. If, however, the lender does not name assets as security to create a real insurance contract, but charges merely for assuming the risk, he is not charging for any real thing, and the contract resolves into a *mutuum* with interest. This latter case is as if the guarantor charged the risk premium without named collateral amounts to the mere promise of the guarantor, not backed up by any particular assets, to repay the loan with interest — which is precisely usury.

---

[38] Cf. Dickson, *Usury: Frequently Asked Questions*, q18, p. 36.

As North claims, it is possible to quite accurately determine the overall level of risk on the extension of credit in *mutuum* loans. That is not to be denied. The mere fact of accurate quantification is not in itself a reason that the quantified thing gives rise to a real basis for a charge. Even Lessius, writing after Medina, provides a certain set of rules to be followed if the title is admitted, one of those being "the charge must not be greater than an independent insurer would make,"[39] which undermines the argument that seeks to justify the mere charge (without real insurance) by the lender, because the borrower could legitimately insure it with a third party.

If the lender acts as both lender and insurer, and the real insurance charge is a condition of borrowing, then the situation resolves without usury. If, however, the lender charges a fee for the risk which is not a real insurance contract, the charge is not for anything real and the contract resolves into usury.

2.3.3 *Inflation*

Thirdly, the inflationary aspect of interest can be summarised as "[the] lender wants to be paid back in money that will purchase as many goods as the money he lent. In an inflationary society, the lender will add a new demand; enough money to compensate him for the expected fall in the value of the nation's circulating media."[40] On the face of it, this seems to be a reasonable expectation. That a lender would be in an impoverished position at the term of the loan by having reduced purchasing power is a fact that can be readily quantified by consumer price indexes, thus giving the claim a quantifiable basis. Claiming something over and above the principal to compensate for this is, therefore, merely returning the lender to his previous position, something which can be argued is required in justice.

---

[39] Noonan, *The Scholastic Analysis of Usury*, 288.
[40] North, *An Introduction to Christian Economics*, 365.

There are three counterarguments to this position. Firstly, things are subject to decay and require labour to preserve and maintain them. Secondly, there is no reason why the price of things should remain stable and that purchasing power should be maintained. Thirdly, circumstances influencing inflation are extrinsic to the loan contract.

First, it is self-evident that all material goods decay sooner or later. Suppose someone lent fresh peaches with an expectation of return in six months.[41] If uneaten, the peaches are going to be rotten within a week. The borrower, by personally guaranteeing to return peaches in six months, is taking "all the risk and labour of providing them"[42] on himself. The borrower can be thought to be contracting out the preservation of his goods, be that peaches or money, because the personal guarantee assures the return, whatever circumstances intervene. On this analysis, if there is any compensation due, it should be from the lender to the borrower for the investment of time and labour in actually preserving the goods from inevitable decay. Now clearly some goods decay more slowly than peaches, but the fact of decay, rather than the rate is the important point.

Second, it is simply question-begging to assert that one's money should be able to buy the same quantity and quality of goods at the term of the loan. There is no reason intrinsic to the loan itself that makes this to be the case. Since the price of goods varies with supply and demand, and since both of these factors are subject to changes, even if one kept the money oneself, purchasing power would not be constant between two time periods. In order to make this argument, one implicitly asserts the premise that a fixed quantity of money must purchase the same goods at different time periods. This is obviously false; money is a measure and the variation in prices is a constant demonstration that money is fulfilling its function.

Third, suppose one admits for argument's sake that one

---

[41] Dickson, *Usury: Frequently Asked Questions*, 59.
[42] Dickson, 59.

ought to be compensated for the effects of inflation. What set of goods, what prices are to be the objective basis for such a claim? Consumer price indexes reflect the changing prices of bundles of popular and common goods, but why should one set of goods be the measure of another? Are milk, eggs, houses, cars, or train tickets the true arbiter? If so, why? What if one could create a price index of all saleable goods? Would this create a just claim? If the index covered everything in the jurisdiction in which the currency can be used, this would be a geographical area far greater than that in which the lender would ever purchase goods, so it is not clear how or why this should be the determinant of any inflationary compensation.

As these three explanations — time preference, risk premium, and compensation for inflation — do not satisfactorily justify interest on a *mutuum*,[43] one might now ask: if one cannot charge interest on a loan of money in a *mutuum*, and yet it is one of the most ubiquitous means of extending credit in any economy, what course of action is there? How can the everyday activity of credit operate within these limits?

---

[43] Note again that these arguments are levelled against the three factors as justification for interest on a *mutuum*, not against them as determinants of commodity prices in a marketplace.

3
IF INTEREST CAN NEVER BE CHARGED, WHAT COURSE OF ACTION IS LEFT?

"THERE has been a tendency to consider the usury prohibition as if it forbade absolutely and in all ways the making of profit through the extension of credit."[1] This is far from the case. The usury prohibition does not cut against the idea that individuals can and should seek legitimate profit; instead, it offers three alternative contracts with limited recourse.

3.1 THE *SOCIETAS* OR PARTNERSHIP

The most widely used type of investment contract is the *societas*, or a partnership agreement. This was made between an investor and a merchant, in which the investor committed money, the merchant labour, and together the two partners shared the profits of the venture. The investor, while retaining ownership of his money, put it at the disposal of the merchant to trade with and generate a profit. This profit, according to the agreement, is the property of both the investor and the merchant, and the investor was entitled to receive a proportion of those profits in relationship to his initial investment.

This contractual arrangement differs in a number of respects from a *mutuum*. It will be helpful here to draw out the relevant points of analysis by considering Noonan's in-depth treatment of Aquinas's argument.[2] Against the

---
[1] Noonan, *The Scholastic Analysis of Usury*, 407.
[2] Cf. Thomas E. Woods Jr., *The Church and the Market: A Catholic Defense of the Free Economy* (Lanham, MD: Lexington Books, 2015), 111–15 as an example of the influence that Noonan's work has on the understanding of usury for contemporary authors. In this short passage, Woods repeats Noonan's analysis almost verbatim as if it were sound both in its reasoning and in its interpretation of Aquinas, neither of which are without problems, as we shall see.

objection that since it is lawful to receive interest on a sum of money lent to a merchant "it is also lawful to receive interest for money lent [*mutuata*],"³ Aquinas argues:

> He that entrusts his money [*committit pecuniam suam*] to a merchant or craftsman so as to form a kind of society [*societatis*], does not transfer the ownership [*dominium*] of his money to them, for it remains his, so that at his risk the merchant speculates with it, or the craftsman...works with it [*vel artifex operatur*], and consequently he may lawfully demand as something belonging to him, part of the profits derived from his money.⁴

There are three claims in this short passage which distinguish the contract of a *societas* from a *mutuum*. First, the investor "that entrusts his money to a merchant...does not transfer ownership of his money." Aquinas's argument against usury is based on the premise that use and ownership of money are not separable. Noonan asserts that "Thomas here abandons his own principle that the use and ownership of money are indistinguishable."⁵ How is this apparent contradiction to be resolved? This relationship between ownership of money and its use is made clear by the following example. Suppose you give a friend £10 to go to the shop to buy wine, and your friend is robbed on the way

---

Woods first demonstrates how ill-equipped he is to enter the debate on usury. Replying to Aquinas's argument that to sell something that does not exist is unjust, Woods simply says "so what?" After following Noonan's argument, he then goes on to claim, with no irony, that "all this inconsistency from so staggering an intellect as that of St. Thomas speaks volumes about the logical difficulties in the prohibition of interest." The much more obvious solution is that the inconsistency sits with Noonan, whom Woods follows closely, in an attempt to justify his position that there is nothing of worth in arguments against usury.

³ Aquinas, *Summa Theologiae: Secunda Secundae*, 1–91, q78, a2, objs.
⁴ Aquinas, II-II, q78, a2, ad5.
⁵ Noonan, *The Scholastic Analysis of Usury*, 143. In the preceding passage, perhaps because Noonan was intent on showing a change in position on usury, he inaccurately reads the word "use" into Aquinas where it is not to be found.

and the money stolen. Does your friend, in justice, owe you £10? The example hinges on whether you intended to buy the wine and the friend is exercising the use of the money on your behalf, or whether your friend intended to buy the wine and borrowed money from you with the intention to pay it back. In the former case your money has been lost by no fault of the friend, who was exercising use on your behalf, and therefore there is no title to claim the money back from him. In the latter case, the friend really became the owner of the money and lost it through circumstance, so in justice really does owe you the money.[6]

In a similar way, in a *societas*, the investor commits his money to the merchant, establishing in law a commercial organisation (which one can think of as the equivalent of a limited company) to which both parties have a claim of ownership. The commitment of funds to the merchant is shorthand for saying that the merchant now has a legal right to dispose of the goods of the partnership including the money. The investor retains ownership insofar as he has a claim on the profit (or loss) of the partnership, and the merchant has a right to make use of the money on behalf of the investor. In this arrangement there is no personal guarantee involved in the return of the money. It is from the fruits of the partnership that the principal is returned. Security on the contract is limited to the assets of the partnership and not to the individual fortune of the merchant.

The second claim is that ownership is determined by the incidence of risk. In a *societas*, if the venture fails, then the investor has no title to claim a return of the principal from the merchant.[7] Again, the security on the contract, the thing

---

[6] It seems clear that where trivial sums are concerned, pity would override the demands of justice between friends and the debt would be counted as nothing. However, for the purposes of a simple example, the analysis is relevant and sheds light on the question of the *apparent* contradiction in Aquinas's premises.

[7] Setting aside for the moment theft, vandalism, fraud, gross negligence and other things which are criminal matters with recourse in law while extrinsic to the contract itself.

that guarantees the return, is not a personal guarantee, but the assets and productivity of the partnership. Herein we see another difference between the *societas* and the *mutuum*, that *res perit dominus* (the thing perishes to the owner). The lender bears the risk of loss on the venture. This stands in contrast to the *mutuum*, where the risk of loss of the goods is borne exclusively by the borrower who must return the principal, whatever happens to the goods.

The third claim is that the criterion of risk is the mark of ownership, but not the source of profit. As Noonan interprets this third claim, "the capitalist is not paid the price of peril."[8] The fundamental question here is from what source does the investor derive a profit? The investor has committed money at his risk. Aquinas asserts that the lender does not profit from the risk, which leaves as the only other option that the lender profits from the use of his money in the partnership. However, some see in the usury analysis that the sterility of money underpins the prohibition. The apparent contradiction is that the investor profits from the use of his money which is sterile, but sterile things do not produce fruit. It is clear, however, if one considers the fact that a *societas* gives rise to a commercial organisation, that the investor has a claim on the property of the organisation, including the money and the profit of the activity of the partnership. Therefore, the gain arising from the ventures of the partnership, as generated through the combination of the money of the investor and the labour of the merchant, is the thing that gives rise to any excess, to which the investor has a right. This is not by way of money giving birth to money, but by way of economic activity giving rise to an increase.

Here we see the Aristotelian concept of the sterility of money at play. If one treats money as sterile, the question is from what source, if not the risk, does the investor take his return? The investor's return comes from the productive output of the enterprise. If one looks at the enterprise as a

---

[8] Noonan, *The Scholastic Analysis of Usury*, 144.

whole, money looks to be fruitful, because the investor has received a return over the principal with no work, so money must be fruitful. It is misleading to focus on the "work" of the investor. He has committed money, at his own risk, to the enterprise, and, therefore owning a share in the enterprise, justly shares in the future returns which are potential at the start of the agreement and become actual later.

Analysis of the nature of a *societas* adds a vital distinction about loans of money, namely that it is possible for Alice to own money and for Bob to use it for her, but not possible for Bob to own money without the right to use it. The incidence of risk and the fact that the investor does not profit from the risk demonstrate that the contract is asset recourse, and those assets are the goods of the partnership. There is no personal guarantee involved.

3.2 THE CENSUS OR CONTRACT OF RENT

"As the *societas* was the most usual contract for capital investment in commerce of animal husbandry, so the *census* was the normal form of investment in land and the regular instrument of state credit."[9] "The contract of *census* or annual revenues was a contract of purchase of the right to receive an annual payment from some property or person."[10] Initially the return was paid in the fruit of the underlying good on which the *census* was raised, while from the twelfth century onwards, it would more commonly be paid in money.[11] This contract is typically translated into English as rent charge.

The *census* is relevant for two reasons. First, because it looks very much like a *mutuum* with interest. A purchaser, taking the role of lender, gives money and receives principal and interest from the seller (taking the role of borrower) who commits to periodic payments. Once redeemed, it resembles a *mutuum* with interest. Second, because with this

---

[9] Noonan, 154.
[10] Dempsey, *Interest and Usury*, 161.
[11] Munro, "The Medieval Origins of the Financial Revolution," 518.

contract (building on analysis of the *societas*) it is possible to more accurately distinguish personally guaranteed lending (*mutuum* lending) from recourse lending in order to place limits on what is and what is not usury.

A typical example of a *census* contract is that of a landowner selling a stream of annual payments, derivable from the produce and fruit of some part of his land. For example, for ten thousand pounds, he gives the purchaser five hundred pounds a year until the contract is redeemed. In order to redeem the contract, the land-owner must buy himself out of it by returning the initial sum. So, at the term of the *census*, the purchaser has received both the principal (the initial sum) and interest, the annual payments. The rent payment is derivable from the produce of the land itself and secures the contract. If the crop fails in a year, then the seller's obligation to make the corresponding payment may be lessened.

> The advantage of the plan [the *census*] was that it enabled owners of lands to borrow for all purposes, among others for the improvement of their estates; while on the other hand, it provided a safe field of investment for individuals and corporations, such as monastic houses, who desired a steady income without the trouble of managing additional property.[12]

There are a variety of types of *census* contract, some resembling a *mutuum* more closely than others. A *real census* was based on the fruit of real property, in contrast with a *personal census* raised on the returns of the future labour of an individual. In between these two positions is a *census* raised by the juridical person of the state on future tax revenues, something closely resembling a modern-day bond. *Census* contracts could also be perpetual or redeemable by either party on demand.

There are two questions to consider: firstly, what is the nature of a *census* contract? And secondly, does this analysis render all such contracts licit, or only some?

---

[12] Ashley, *Introduction to English Economic History and Theory*, 406.

The standard answer to the first question was that it was a sale, and three alternatives were proposed for the thing that was being sold: "either, the money paid as a return; or the right to the money paid as a return; or, interest in the property producing the return."[13]

The minority opinion was the first case, in which it was asserted that money is sold for money. This opinion did not gain traction among commentators. The primary reason for the opposition was that "money, which is formally non-vendible, is sold."[14] This is to say that since money is the middle term in exchange, it cannot be treated as something that can be sold in its own right. Juan de Lugo (1583–1660), a Spanish Jesuit theologian and philosopher, would reiterate the same argument almost a century later: the contract of *census* is not justified "by the fact that present money is exchanged for future money which is of less value, for this would justify usury for the same reason."[15] If money is treated as a commodity, it is unique in that it has an inherent measure and therefore any sale of money can only be at its face value. In the same vein, time-preference, risk, and inflation do not give rise to a real basis to price money as anything other than its face value in a *mutuum*, which leaves two other alternatives to analyse.

These two other alternatives are the right to money paid as a return, or interest in the property producing the return. The latter can be restated as a claim in the underlying property producing the return. On analysis, these two positions collapse into one another.

As de Lugo explains:

> Part of the usufruct of the field on which the census is constituted is bought. Then . . . by another contract, which is implicitly contained in the very constitution of a real census, it is agreed by the parties

---

[13] Noonan, *The Scholastic Analysis of Usury*, 155.
[14] Henry of Ghent, *Quodlibetales* (Paris, 1518), Q8:24, cited in Noonan, 155.
[15] Dempsey, *Interest and Usury*, 171.

> that, for the hope of the fruit which the buyer has from that usufruct, the seller binds himself to pay such an annual payment of money; and in this way the prior contract is reduced to the obligation of paying only an annual sum, by which the seller redeems the partial usufruct of the field which he had sold; the field itself, however, remaining really obliged in the manner of a pledge for the payment of the promised money...[16]

That is to say, the purchaser of the *census* buys part of the fruit (the usufruct) of the field. Rather than take this payment as the actual fruit such as wheat, barley, or whatever, "by another contract... implicitly contained in very constitution of a real *census*" the seller "binds himself" to pay in cash "an annual sum." In so doing, the purchaser is redeeming his part of the fruit of the field. Importantly Lugo argues that "the field itself remain[s] really obliged in the manner of a pledge for the payment." That is to say, the field acts as the security on the *census* and it is the fruit of the field, the property on which the *census* is raised, that is the ultimate source of the return.

This can be further developed by considering the nature of ownership of property. One can have title to a certain piece of property in three ways: i. by outright ownership and dominion ("the right of exclusive control and disposal over a thing at will"[17]), ii. by having certain limited rights over the property (such as right of use without dominion), or iii. virtually (as with the right to an inheritance which prior to inheriting is potential and not yet actual).

In the *census* contract, raised on some underlying good, be that a farm, future tax revenues, or a person, one is not selling a piece of property with dominion over it, as the *census* seller retains ownership. Nor is the *census* the sale of a merely virtual right, as the contract creates a claim

---

[16] Juan de Lugo, *Disputationes*, 27:2:17, cited in Noonan, *The Scholastic Analysis of Usury*, 242.
[17] Fagothey, *Right and Reason*, 368.

for the purchaser over the underlying property itself. This leaves certain limited rights over the property, the right to a certain share in the usufruct which, as Lugo describes, the purchaser agrees is to be paid by a fixed amount periodically. In this way, the two alternatives collapse into each other. The purchaser buys a limited share in the property producing the return (the third alternative) and contracts with the seller that the fruit from the property is returned in the form of money (the second alternative).

As a consequence of the property interest in the underlying goods, the purchaser has a right to money paid as a return. It is as if the seller is paying rent (hence the translation to rent charge) on the good in proportion to the share of the purchaser's claim on the underlying asset. This is called asset recourse lending, in that the liability of the seller is limited to the specific goods on which the *census* is raised. It stands in contrast to a *mutuum*, wherein the borrower personally guarantees repayment without any property as security. This also provides a principle to determine which *census* contracts are licit or otherwise.

A personal redeemable *census* most closely resembles a *mutuum* because in such a contract an individual sells for a lump sum a stream of future payments derivable from his own labour. That is, the seller makes himself the security on the contract. At the point at which such a contract is redeemed, the seller has received both principal and interest back. From this position it becomes apparent why the personal *census* was generally understood to be an illicit contract.

In purchasing a *census*, one purchases a property interest in the underlying good. The underlying good in a personal *census* is the person and in that sense ceases to be lending backed by some real security; instead, it is full recourse lending, with the borrower personally on the hook to cover the debt. Full recourse lending with interest to a borrower is precisely a *mutuum* loan, and it has already been shown that interest on a *mutuum* loan is to sell what does not exist and is unjust (excepting extrinsic titles). A personal *census*, then, differs categorically from a *census* raised on some real good because on analysis the security is a personal guarantee, rather than some real asset.[18] For this reason, it reduces to a *mutuum* (a personally guaranteed loan) and therefore deriving interest from it is illicit and unjust.

Here it can be seen that the nature of the security in the contract can determine the type of contract. While superficially a *census* can look like a *mutuum*, once one looks more closely at the specific goods the contract governs, it becomes more clearly a distinct contract in the case of the exchange based on some real underlying goods, or reduces to a *mutuum* when there is no security, and the borrower is only personally guaranteeing repayment.

With the *census* in mind, it is possible to make a distinction using the concept of the personal guarantee and more precisely delineate the scope of the usury analysis. Speaking equivocally, there are two types of person that can personally guarantee a loan of any kind: a natural person and a juridical person. A natural person is Anna, Bob, or Clare. These are individual human persons. A juridical person is any business, association, group, or corporation that exists in law with its associated rights and duties. Natural persons can be members of juridical persons, but are distinct and separable from them.

When a natural person gives a personal guarantee in a *mutuum* and then defaults, there are no assets forming security on the loan; the lender has recourse only to the person of the borrower to make good the debt. If a juridical person gives a personal guarantee in a *mutuum* and then

---

[18] The bull *Cum Onus* (1568) of Pius V lends magisterial weight to this distinction: "We by this our constitution decree, that rent or an annuity, can by no means be created, or constituted, unless in an immovable thing, or a thing that may be considered as immovable, of its own nature fruitful, and that may be nominally designated by certain limits." Quoted in Jeremiah O'Callaghan, *Usury; or, Lending at Interest; Also, The Exaction and Payment of Certain Church-Fees, Such as Pew-Rents, Burial-Fees, and the like, Together with Forestalling Traffick* (London: William Cobbett, 1828), 83.

defaults, since the juridical person is a bundle of rights and duties associated with particular pieces of property which in law it owns *qua* juridical person, there are real assets behind the personal guarantee which can be recovered to make good the debt. Conceptually, this means that a juridical person cannot enter into a *mutuum* loan. Rather, *mutuum* loans personally guaranteed by a juridical person ought to be thought of as *census* contracts raised on the assets owned by the organisation.

One might object and say that if the personal guarantee of a juridical person is reducible to the assets of that organisation, then the personal guarantee of a natural person ought to reduce to the assets of the natural person. The difference between the two is that a juridical person is *nothing other* than the rights and duties associated with particular pieces of property according to law. It is a legal construct. A natural person is no such thing: a natural person is Alice, Bob, or Clare, who cannot under any analysis be reduced to merely the sum of the property which they own.

There are, therefore, two different contracts for asset-backed lending to juridical persons. One is a *census* raised on a juridical person, which is the receipt of money in exchange for a claim on the fruits of the underlying asset, such as government bonds giving rise to a return from future tax revenues. Alternatively, a business may raise cash by borrowing from a lender and repaying the principal plus interest in a construct that reduces to a *societas*. The source for the interest in both situations is the underlying goods which the juridical persons have a title to. Neither involve personal guarantees from individuals.

3.3 THE TRIPLE CONTRACT

The *contractus trinus*, or triple contract, is relevant to the usury debate on the one hand because it demonstrates innovation in agreements with a view to avoiding usury, and on the other because Noonan claims that it undermines two vital principles of the natural law case against usury — "the position that an investor must run a risk to make a profit and that money must be considered unfruitful,"[19] ultimately undermining the whole case against usury.

It has already been observed that the sterility or fruitfulness of money, by itself, is not an essential part of the Scholastic case against usury. Suitable analysis of the triple contract will demonstrate that the concept of risk is more nuanced than Noonan recognises.

As early as 1486, an overall description of the triple contract can be found, but it was not until Johann Eck (1486–1543) in 1515 that the three implicit agreements were described separately. The first is a *societas*. The second is an insurance contract provided by the merchant to cover the investor against the loss of capital, effectively guaranteeing the return of the principal (via the security forming the insurance) if the venture fails. Finally, there is a contract for "the sale of an uncertain gain for a certain."[20] This third contract is also described by de Roover[21] and Cleary[22] as an insurance contract on a fixed return.

Each contract considered individually poses no challenge for the usury position. "A man could enter into partnership [*societas*] with B; he could insure himself with C against the loss of his capital; and he could insure himself with D against fluctuations in the rate of profit [sale of an uncertain gain for certain]. If all this was morally justifiable, why should not A make the three contracts with the same man B?"[23] As Lessius argues,[24] freedom of contract should

---

[19] Noonan, *The Scholastic Analysis of Usury*, 202.
[20] This is a quotation from the sixteenth-century theologian and philosopher John Major, in his response to Eck. Ashley, *An Introduction to English Economic History and Theory*, 445.
[21] Raymond de Roover, "Scholastic Economics: Survival and Lasting Influence from the Sixteenth Century to Adam Smith," *The Quarterly Journal of Economics* 69, no. 2 (1955): 173.
[22] Cleary claims correctly that "insurance against loss of profit was usually spoken of as a 'sale of an uncertain gain for certain,'" quoting Ashley's reference to Major verbatim. Cleary, *The Church and Usury: An Essay on Some Historical and Theological Aspects of Money Lending*, 127.
[23] Ashley, *An Introduction to English Economic History and Theory*, 440.
[24] Cf. Wim Decock, "Knowing before Judging. Law and Economic

not prevent these contracts being concluded between only two parties.

The triple contract, then, is an agreement in which an investor forms a *societas* with a merchant, while guaranteeing a fixed return (interest) over the principal. The difficulty that requires a resolution is that "each individual contract was valid but when combined simulated a risk-free loan."[25] Both Noonan's analysis[26] and, more recently, DeCock's[27] are based on an equivocation on the nature of insurance contracts. The merchant has two options for the insurance contract. He can name real assets as security for the insurance.[28] In this case, if the venture fails to produce a profit and make good the investor's principal and interest, those assets can be liquidated to pay the debt. Alternatively, the merchant does not name any assets as security for the insurance. This makes the insurance a mere promise, rather than a contract terminating in real assets. If the venture fails, the merchant is personally liable to cover the principal and interest. In this case, the triple contract is nothing other than a legal fiction.[29] The promise of insurance is just like a personal guarantee in that the contract terminates in a person rather than assets. The distinction of three contracts in this scenario vanishes and one is left with a promise by the borrower (the merchant) to repay principal and interest, precisely a *mutuum* with interest. This is usury.

Analysis in Early Modern Jesuit Ethics," *Journal of Markets and Morality* 21 (2018): 315–19.

[25] Jared Rubin, "Institutions, the Rise of Commerce and the Persistence of Laws: Interest Restrictions in Islam and Christianity," *The Economic Journal* 121, no. 557 (2011): 1314n10.

[26] Noonan, *The Scholastic Analysis of Usury*, 201–29.

[27] In Decock, "Knowing before Judging," the equivocation is merely implied and not explicit, but this lack of clarity opens up the opportunity for misunderstanding.

[28] This does raise the question of why a merchant would need to provide real security in order to raise money. The simple answer is that his ready cash is tied up in illiquid assets, either land, property, or some other venture, which he then uses as a pledge to raise money.

[29] See section 2.3.2 on risk.

Noonan claims that the investor must run a risk. The innovation in the triple contract is a genuine development. Interest on a *mutuum* is guaranteed by a person, but interest in a (genuine) triple contract is backed by the success of the venture *or* named assets under a real insurance contract. The latter avoids a construction that would make it usurious. The incidence of risk as discussed by Noonan as a key determinant in the debate is not relevant. The construction of the triple contract effectively diminishes the risk to the investor by way of an insurance contract. The insurance guarantees the return of the principal via a limited recourse agreement, thereby avoiding usury. Of course, there is still risk that the named assets may be stolen or destroyed; the risk can never be removed completely, but one can reduce the overall risk of not making a return.[30]

It can be noted that what is common to these three contracts and distinguishes them from a *mutuum* is that the recourse is limited to specific real assets. In the *societas*, it is the property and assets of the partnership that are used by the merchant. If the business fails, the merchant has no obligation to return the principal and any surplus to the investor. In the *census*, the return is paid from the fruit of the underlying good on which the contract is raised, and if the underlying good produces no fruit in a given period, the seller has no obligation to the purchaser. In the triple contract, it is *either* the assets of the partnership, as in the case of the *societas*, *or* the named assets underlying the real insurance contract if the venture fails, that secure the return. Triple contracts without a real insurance contract reduce to a mere personal guarantee of insurance which is nothing other than a *mutuum*.

---

[30] Noonan equivocates on the nature of risk: the insurance contract removes the risk that the investor fails to make a return, but it does nothing to the underlying risk of this or that venture that he invests in. The same risk with respect to the particular enterprise is run in a *societas* or a *triple contract*. What the *triple contract* does by its construction is mitigate the impact on the investor in the event that the risk actually happens (be that fire, pirates, shipwreck, locusts, whatever).

Lewis Watt, writing on usury in the early twentieth century, says of the theory as it stood at the middle of the eighteenth century:

> [the] position was so fundamentally sound, and at the same time so capable of being adapted to the development of economic conditions, that it might have been accepted not only by moralists but also by economists and jurists with great benefit to public welfare, material as well as moral.[31]

That this endorsement summarises nearly five hundred years of European economic history and concerns a position against usury deemed not only to be plausible but credible across such a wide expanse of geography, economic realities, and contributors, leaves little doubt as to the strength of the fundamental theses that animated the discussion.

---

[31] Lewis Watt, *Usury in Catholic Theology* (Oxford: Catholic Social Guild, 1963), 34. The lectures that served as the basis of this book, which first appeared in 1945, were given in 1937.

4
DOES USURY REALLY DESERVE OUR ATTENTION?

Having established what usury is, where it can occur, and alternative means of loaning and investing that fall outside the usury rubric, one may well be tempted to ask if this is merely of theoretical interest without any practical relevance. When a practice is so ubiquitous that seemingly nothing can be done about it, is there really any reason to take the theory seriously? I believe the answer is a decisive yes. For, if we make use of the concept of the personal guarantee inherent in a *mutuum*, we shall see that usury entails a form of slavery—a slavery no less worthy of elimination than any other form of slavery.[1]

4.1 INTEREST ON A *MUTUUM* IMPLIES THE BORROWER IS THE LENDER'S PROPERTY

The first stage of the argument is seen via the following syllogism. Interest on a *mutuum* is an attempt to profit directly from the personal guarantee. The personal guarantee gives the lender recourse to the borrower himself. Therefore, to profit from a *mutuum* is to profit from the use of another person. It is important to look at each of these premises in turn.

Observe that one must have a real title to something in order to use it as one's own property. A title is a bundle of rights in a piece of property and "is the reason why [a] particular concrete right exists. Its purpose is to establish a connection between the subject and the matter of the right."[2] For example, one could inherit land which would give one rights over it, to sell it, build on it, restrict access to it, etc. One

---

[1] Cf. Dickson, *Usury: Frequently Asked Questions*, 33: "Usury is in the same moral genus as slavery."
[2] Fagothey, *Right and Reason*, 201.

could purchase a car, and one's title over the car would be given on the basis of the contract of sale. Or one could pawn some property in order to borrow money for a time, and the pawnbroker would have a title, a right to the property, to sell the pawn if the borrower failed to repay the money on time.

Prescinding from two extrinsic titles, in a *mutuum* as such there is nothing to give rise to an interest charge. The only thing exchanged in a *mutuum* is the personal guarantee in return for the principal, to which the lender has a claim. This can be thought of as a right to a certain sum of money at a certain date. Since this personal guarantee, a promise convertible to cash at the term of the loan, is the only thing the lender has a claim to, it can be the only source for his claim to profit (i.e., interest). Therefore, a *mutuum* with interest is an attempt to profit from a personal guarantee.

The minor premise is that the personal guarantee gives the lender recourse to the borrower. A *mutuum* authorises the borrower to consume in use the property lent, while personally guaranteeing that he will restore an equivalent to the lender at the term of the loan.[3] Now security on a contract is those specified assets that are pledged as collateral to guarantee that the contracting parties fulfil their obligations. Since the *mutuum* authorises the borrower to consume in use the property lent, the specific money lent cannot be security on the contract. This is because once the property has been consumed or alienated, neither of the parties will have any title to that specific property. With no title to it, it cannot be the subject of any rights of either the borrower or the lender. If the property loaned in a *mutuum* cannot be the thing that secures the performance of the contract, the only other thing that can secure it is the promise, the personal guarantee, of the borrower to repay the loan. However, this promise or personal guarantee does not exist as something distinct from the borrower himself.[4] Therefore the personal guar-

---

[3] Dickson, *Usury: Frequently Asked Questions*, 54–57.
[4] Dickson, 54–77.

antee gives the lender recourse to the borrower himself, and anything he does own or could own, for principal and interest.

So, the profit is derived from the personal guarantee, and the personal guarantee is recourse to the borrower himself. Therefore, to profit on a *mutuum* is to profit from a person. Now, it is self-evident that one can profit only from the use of one's own property. If this were not the case, the ludicrous result would follow that one could, for one's own gain, dispose of property owned exclusively by another person. Therefore, in profiting from a person, the lender is treating the person as his property.

4.2 DISTINGUISHING TWO FORMS OF SLAVERY

Two kinds of relationship fall under the general concept of slavery. Slavery can be divided into chattel slavery and just title slavery. The former is the more common idea of slavery, typified by forcible kidnapping, transportation, sale, and subsequent lifetime of hard labour of individuals. The latter is a different conception, present throughout history, in which one person claims the right to the service of another for an extended period of time.

Chattel slavery signifies "a social and economic institution in which one human being is the legal property of another, or, as the condition of such a human being who thus become a *res non persona*, a human chattel without rights or privileges."[5]

In history, it was not uncommon for the masters of such slaves "to determine where he or she lived and how much he or she was fed and clothed; to restrict his or her education; to pledge him or her for a loan, forfeit him or her for a default, sell him or her for cash; to do the same as to his or her offspring; and to discipline him or her by physical punishments if he or she were rude or boisterous or slack

---

[5] C. Williams, "Slavery, II (and the Church)," *New Catholic Encyclopaedia* (Washington, DC: Catholic University of America, 2003), 207.

in service."⁶ Indeed, the owner "frequently had the right to control his [the slave's] physical reproduction."⁷

Thus, the institution of slavery is manifested in the total control and disposal the owner has over another individual at will. Chattel slaves are treated as mere property by their owners. It is an historical fact that owners of chattel slaves acted towards their slave as they would dispose of any other piece of property, with all the abuse of individuals that this entailed. While it is not essential to chattel slavery that all manner of abuse be part of the relationship, historically this was so normal in practice that it is hard to separate the idea and the reality distinctly. The practice is manifestly a very grave injustice and rightly outlawed.⁸

Just title slavery, on the other hand, is a different type of relationship between individuals, one which "does not abolish the natural equality of men."⁹ "Since it is obviously morally unproblematic for one person to come to owe another this or that particular service as a matter of right, it is in principle possible that someone could come legitimately to owe another service for some prolonged period of time, perhaps even a lifetime."¹⁰ That is to say, in order

---

[6] John T. Noonan, "Development in Moral Doctrine," *Theological Studies* 54 (1993): 664.
[7] Richard Hellie, "Slavery," in *Encyclopaedia Britannica*, August 2020, www.britannica.com/topic/slavery-sociology.
[8] "Slavery as a historical institution looked on slaves as property, as animated tools, to be bought and sold. There can hardly be anything more degrading to human dignity or more destructive of human rights than this revolting practice. There can be no possible moral defense for slave hunting, nor for letting children be born into slavery, and what begins unjustly and in bad faith cannot be righted by the mere passage of time. That the civilized world accepted this institution for so long illustrates the slow growth of moral social consciousness and the difficulty of seeing remote conclusions of the natural law." Fagothey, *Right and Reason*, 201.
[9] Cardinal Gerdil (*Comp. Instit. Civil.*, L, vii), cited in James J. Fox, "Slavery, Ethical Aspect of," in *The Catholic Encyclopaedia* (New York: The Encyclopedia Press, 1913), 40.
[10] Edward Feser, "Classical Natural Law Theory, Property Rights, and Taxation," *Social Philosophy and Policy* 27, no. 1 (2010): 37–38, n42.

to repay a debt really owed, entering into a relationship in which the debt is repaid through labour is not *per se* morally problematic.

This may well come about in circumstances other than those prevalent today. "In the poverty of previous times most people would have preferred to have the basic necessities of life met, such as having enough food to eat—though it was earned in freely chosen service to another—than to starve to death in their liberty."[11] The services that one man can legitimately offer to another and which are typically remunerated in an employment contract could come to be owed under other circumstances—for example, offering to another the service of labour in return for shelter and food to avoid destitution.

This allows us to see the essence of just title slavery wherein "one man is understood to become subject to the dominion of another to the extent that the master has a perpetual right to all those services which one man may justly perform for another."[12] Note that, just as with an employment contract, the employer has limitations on what he can demand of the employee, i.e., he cannot justly demand the employee perform actions intrinsically inimical to his own interests,[13] and this same principle is demanded in the relationship of just title slavery, drawing from recognition of the natural equality of men.[14]

---

[11] Joel S. Panzer, *The Popes and Slavery* (New York: Alba House, 1996), 4.

[12] Cardinal Gerdil (*Comp. Instit. Civil.*, L, vii), cited in Fox, "Slavery, Ethical Aspect of," 40.

[13] For example, if one employed a chef, the fact that he spends his time cooking for you is not *per se* inimical to his own good, even though he could be doing something else with his time, which he may well prefer. Expecting dinner is perfectly reasonable in light of the employment contract. Demanding that the chef chop off his own arm and serve it for dinner, however, is *in itself* contrary to the innate good of the chef, i.e., intrinsically inimical, and it would be unjust to demand this.

[14] This principle is seen in the Geneva Convention with respect to another form of just title slavery, penal servitude. The convention limits the conditions with which conquering powers can utilise the

In distinguishing these two types of slavery, two ideas emerge. The essence of chattel slavery is the treatment of the slave merely as property. The essence of just title slavery is the right to the services of a slave who discharges a real obligation. While this gives some framework on the limits of ownership as it pertains to other people, it is worth noting "that even the more limited form of servitude natural law allows in principle [just title slavery] is so morally hazardous that in practice it cannot be justified."[15]

4.3 USURY AS FINANCIAL CHATTEL SLAVERY

Having first established that the lender treats the borrower as his property in charging interest on a *mutuum*, and now having established that the essence of chattel slavery is the state of an individual being treated as property by another, it is clear that *by definition* the very act of charging interest on a *mutuum* is a form of chattel slavery.

One may object: since chattel slavery has historically been characterised by the total subjugation of individuals, typified by forced reproduction, while borrowers who pay interest retain their liberty and every other freedom, the conclusion must be false. This objection fails to make the necessary distinction. Chattel slavery is defined as the treatment of another as one's property. The characteristics typically associated with the institution are not the essence of slavery.

However, for the avoidance of doubt, we might say that usury is a species of chattel slavery, then distinguish between the historical form of chattel slavery and this form of chattel slavery brought about by usury (interest-bearing *mutua*). Both treat individuals as property, but to differentiate the two types, we can call the latter "financial chattel slavery"

---

labour of prisoners of war, including their working conditions, the degree of danger, the duration of daily labour, their pay, their medical condition. Cf. "Convention (III) Relative to the Treatment of Prisoners of War. (Geneva)," 6 U. S. T. 3316; 75 U. N. T. S. 135 § (1949) Part III, Section III, Articles 49–57.

[15] Feser, "Classical Natural Law Theory, Property Rights, and Taxation," 38n42.

insofar as with chattel slavery many or all of the rights attaching to ownership are exercised over the slave, while in financial chattel slavery only limited rights attaching to ownership are exercised.[16]

To develop this further, we can compare it to owning shares in a company. With a small fraction of overall shares, no one would claim to own the company in the sense that he could direct the employees' work, make decisions about what the company does and does not do, and so forth. However, one clearly exercises some right of ownership in the company in making a return via the shares. In the same way, an interest-bearing *mutuum* is far from total control and ownership of a person, but one exercises a right of ownership over the lender in deriving a profit from him via interest on the loan.

Calvin Elliot describes the effect of these differences well:

> Not only does financial slavery exact more labor for the amount invested, but it is more heartless than chattel bondage. The master has a personal interest in the [chattel] slave he bought. His health and strength was an object of care and his death a great loss.... The usurer has no personal interest in his slave. He has no care for his health or his life; they are of no interest to him. He may live in a distant state and has no anxiety about those who service him. Their personal ills give him no concern.[17]

There is of course a moral asymmetry in the circumstances of contracting for slavery. A borrower may enter into a contract in which he is made the slave of the lender (willingly or unwillingly, knowingly or unknowingly) to achieve some good end,[18] e.g., to repay a debt or to buy a house with

---

[16] The League of Nations Slavery Convention defines slavery as "the status or condition of a person over whom any or all of the powers attaching to the right of ownership are exercised." "Slavery Convention," 60 LNTS 253 § (1926) Article 1.1. Note the inclusion of "any" in the definition, not just "all."
[17] Elliot, *Usury: A Scriptural, Ethical and Economic View*, 83.
[18] Aquinas, *Summa Theologiae: Secunda Secundae*, 1–91, q78, a4.

a mortgage which he could not otherwise afford.[19] On the part of the lender, however, the act of lending which entails enslaving the borrower does not have this neutral moral character. Consider that to surrender one's possessions to avoid physical harm when being mugged is not a moral fault; however, the act of mugging and stealing from another is clearly a moral failing. In the same way, if a person or business actively seeks to lend and contract with another such a debt that he enslaves the borrower for an extended period to repay that debt, it should rightly be thought of as malicious.

Again, one may object: to pursue the line of thought just expounded is to condemn "the economy." If one seriously follows this line of thinking, then the whole economy would need to be upended and replaced. Often horror dawns on the interlocutor as the only apparent alternative is "a return to the Middle Ages." It should be clear from what has been said that this is not the correct conclusion to draw. Usury, properly understood, is not a feature of every financial transaction. The simple way of spotting whether there is usury in a transaction is with the following three questions:[20]

1. Is the loan personally guaranteed?
2. Is the thing loaned treated as fungible?
3. Is profitable interest charged?

If the answer to each is yes, then there is usury. In answering the third question, one must keep in mind that neither *lucrum cessans* nor the economic justification of time preference, risk, or inflation are just titles. Claims for interest based on these would be profitable interest.

To make the practical implications of these arguments explicit: personally guaranteed lending such as student loans, mortgages, consumer credit, payday loans, credit card

---

[19] Note that personally guaranteed mortgages are a mix of asset-recourse lending and *mutuum* lending, insofar as the bank has recourse to the house first and then to the individual borrower in the case that repossession and sale of the house results in a deficiency (positive outstanding balance after foreclosure) on the mortgage.
[20] Adapted from Dickson, *Usury: Frequently Asked Questions*, q57.

lending, etc., which are all secured by a personal guarantee of the borrower, are interest-bearing *mutuum* loans, and the preceding analysis applies to them. This implies that very many individuals are being treated as property, as slaves of lending institutions.

Once one sees that a *mutuum* with interest is to sell something that does not exist, these conclusions follow. Neither philosophical-legal counterarguments nor economic positions undermine Aquinas's foundational argument and arguments developed from it. This being true, it becomes plain that in charging interest the lender treats the borrower as his property, which is a species of chattel slavery. Through usury, chattel slavery has re-emerged with an appearance different from that of its historical predecessor—it is financial chattel slavery. This conclusion opens up many further questions, not least: What specific fundamental changes in philosophical analysis between the Middle Ages and the present day brought about this change and the gradual acceptance of usury? How has it come to be the case that vast swathes of the population are treated as property by the capital-owning classes through interest-bearing *mutua* without causing an effective revolution?[21] But perhaps the more compelling question, which really does take some imagination, is: what are the alternatives and the innovations that would arise as a result of eliminating usurious lending? These are not questions to be ignored, but questions which demand collective attention and action.

---

[21] One might indeed maintain that the communist revolutions of recent centuries and the constant pressure for increased socialism in modern Western societies are more or less conscious reactions against financial chattel slavery, even if the cure is worse than the disease due to the evils of dispossessing citizens of private property and/or attempting to make the government the owner, manager, and provider of all goods. On the inherent inhumanity of the communist and socialist "solutions," and on capitalism's responsibility for driving them forward, the Catholic social magisterium remains incisive: see Leo XIII's *Rerum Novarum* and Pius XI's *Quadragesimo Anno*.

APPENDICES

I

INSTITUTES
Justinian

BOOK III. TITLE XIV. OF REAL CONTRACTS, OR THE MODES IN WHICH OBLIGATIONS ARE CONTRACTED BY DELIVERY

Real contracts, or contracts concluded by delivery, are exemplified by loan for consumption, that is to say, loan of such things as are estimated by weight, number, or measure; for instance, wine, oil, corn, coined money, copper, silver, or gold: things in which we transfer our property on condition that the receiver shall transfer to us, at a future time, not the same things, but other things of the same kind and quality: and this contract is called *mutuum*, because thereby *meum*, or mine, becomes *tuum*, or thine. The action to which it gives rise is called a condiction.

Again, a man is bound by a real obligation if he takes what is not owed him from another who pays him by mistake; and the latter can, as plaintiff, bring a condiction against him for its recovery, after the analogy of the action whose formula ran "if it be proved that he ought to convey," exactly as if the defendant had received a loan from him. Consequently a pupil who, by mistake, is paid something which is not really owed him without his guardian's authority, will no more be bound by a condiction for the recovery of money not owed than by one for money received as a loan: though this kind of liability does not seem to be founded on contract; for a payment made in order to discharge a debt is intended to extinguish, not to create, an obligation.

So too a person to whom a thing is lent for use is laid under a real obligation, and is liable to the action on a loan for use. The difference between this case and a loan for consumption is considerable, for here the intention is not to make the object lent the property of the borrower, who accordingly is bound to restore the same identical thing. Again, if the receiver of a loan for consumption loses what he has received by some accident, such as fire, the fall of a building, shipwreck, or the attack of thieves or enemies, he still remains bound: but the borrower for use, though responsible for the greatest care in keeping what is lent him—and it is not enough that he has shown as much care as he usually bestows on his own affairs, if only someone else could have been more diligent in the charge of it—has not to answer for loss occasioned by fire or accident beyond his control, provided it did not occur through any fault of his own. Otherwise, of course, it is different: for instance, if you choose to take with you on a journey a thing which has been lent to you for use, and lose it by being attacked by enemies or thieves, or by a shipwreck, it is beyond question that you will be liable for its restoration. A thing is not properly said to be lent for use if any recompense is received or agreed upon for the service; for where this is the case, the use of the thing is held to be hired, and the contract is of a different kind, for a loan for use ought always to be gratuitous.

Again, the obligation incurred by a person with whom a thing is deposited for custody is real, and he can be sued by the action of the deposit; he too being responsible for the restoration of the identical thing deposited, though only where it is lost through some positive act of commission on his part: for carelessness, that is to say, inattention and negligence, he is not liable. Thus a person from whom a thing is stolen, in the charge of which he has been most careless, cannot be called to account, because, if a man entrusts property to the custody of a careless friend, he has no one to blame but himself for his want of caution.

Finally, the creditor who takes a thing in pledge is under a real obligation and is bound to restore the thing itself by the action of pledge. A pledge, however, is for the benefit of both parties; of the debtor, because it enables him to borrow more easily, and of the creditor, because he has the better security for repayment; and accordingly, it is a settled rule that the pledgee cannot be held responsible for more than the greatest care in the custody of the pledge; if he shows this, and still loses it by some accident, he himself is freed from all liability, without losing his right to sue for the debt.[1]

Liber. III, Titulus. XIV. Quibus modis re contrahitur obligatio

Re contrahitur obligatio veluti mutui datione. mutui autem obligatio in his rebus consistit, quae pondere numero mensurave constant, veluti vino oleo frumento pecunia numerata aere argento auro, quas res aut numerando aut metiendo aut pendendo in hoc damus, ut accipientium fiant et quandoque nobis non eaedem res, sed aliae eiusdem naturae et qualitatis reddantur. unde etiam mutuum appellatum sit, quia ita a me tibi datur, ut ex meo tuum fiat. ex eo contractu nascitur actio quae vocatur condictio. Is quoque, qui non debitum accepit ab eo qui per errorem solvit, re obligatur: daturque agenti contra eum propter repetitionem condicticia action. nam proinde ei condici potest "si paret eum dare oportere" ac si mutuum accepisset: unde pupillus, si ei sine tutoris auctoritate non debitum per errorem datum est, non tenetur indebiti condictiones non magis quam mutui datione. sed haec species obligationis non videtur ex contractu consistere, cum is qui solvendi animo dat magis distrahere voluit negotium quam contrahere.

Item is cui res aliqua utenda datur, id est commodatur, re obligatur et tenetur commodati actione. sed is ab eo qui mutuum accepit longe distat: namque non ita res datur, ut eius fiat. et ob id de ea re ipsa restituenda tenetur. et is quidem qui mutuum accepit, si quolibet fortuito casu quod accepit amiserit, veluti incendio ruina naufragio aut latronum hostiumve incursu, nihilo minus obligatus permanet. at is qui utendum accepit sane quidem exactam diligentiam custodiendae rei praestare iubetur nec sufficit ei tantam diligentiam adhibuisse. quantam suis rebus adhibere solitus

---

[1] Justinian, *The Institutes of Justinian*, 130–32.

est, si modo alius diligentior poterit eam rem custodire: sed propter maiorem vim maioresve casus non tenetur, si modo non huius culpa is casus intervenerit: alioquin si id quod tibi commodatum est peregre ferre tecum malueris et vel incursu hostium praedonumve vel naufragio amiseris, dubium non est, quin de restituenda ea re tenearis. commodata autem res tunc proprie intellegitur, si nulla mercede accepta vel constituta res tibi utenda data est. alioquin mercede interveniente locatus tibi usus rei videtur: gratuitum enim debet esse commodatum.

Praeterea et is, apud quem res aliqua deponitur, re obligatur et actione depositi, qui et ipse de ea re quam accepit restituenda tenetur. sed is ex eo solo tenetur, si quid dolo commiserit, culpae autem nomine, id est desidiae atque neglegentiae, non tenetur: itaque securus est qui parum diligenter custoditam rem furto amisit, quia, qui neglegenti amico rem custodiendam tradit, suae facilitati id imputare debet.

Creditor quoque qui pignus accepit re obligatur, qui et ipse de ea ipsa re quam accepit restituenda tenetur actione pigneraticia. sed quia pignus utriusque gratia datur, et debitoris, quo magis ei pecunia crederetur, et creditoris, quo magis ei in tuto sit creditum, placuit sufficere, quod ad eam rem custodiendam exactam diligentiam adhiberet: quam si praestiterit et aliquo fortuito casu rem amiserit, securum esse nec impediri creditum petere.[2]

---

[2] Justinian, *Imperatoris Iustiniani Institutionum, Libri Quattuor*, 392–98.

2

SUMMA THEOLOGIAE, IIAIIAE
St. Thomas Aquinas

QUESTION 78: THE SIN OF USURY

We must now consider the sin of usury, which is committed in loans: and under this head there are four points of inquiry.

1. Whether it is a sin to take money as a price for money lent, which is to receive usury?

2. Whether it is lawful to lend money for any other kind of consideration, by way of payment for the loan?

3. Whether a man is bound to restore just gains derived from money taken in usury?

4. Whether it is lawful to borrow money under a condition of usury?

Article 1: Whether it is a sin to take usury for money lent?

Objection 1: It would seem that it is not a sin to take usury for money lent. For no man sins through following the example of Christ. But Our Lord said of Himself (Luke 19:23): "At My coming I might have exacted it, i.e., the money lent, with usury." Therefore it is not a sin to take usury for lending money.

Obj. 2: Further, according to Ps. 18:8, "The law of the Lord is unspotted," because, to wit, it forbids sin. Now usury of a kind is allowed in the Divine law, according to Deut. 23:19, 20: "Thou shalt not fenerate to thy brother money, nor corn, nor any other thing, but to the stranger": nay more, it is even promised as a reward for the observance of the Law, according to Deut. 28:12: Thou shalt fenerate to many nations, and shalt not borrow of any one. Therefore it is not a sin to take usury.

Obj. 3: Further, in human affairs justice is determined by civil laws. Now civil law allows usury to be taken. Therefore it seems to be lawful.

Obj. 4: Further, the counsels are not binding under sin. But, among other counsels we find (Luke 6:35): "Lend, hoping for nothing thereby." Therefore it is not a sin to take usury.

Obj. 5: Further, it does not seem to be in itself sinful to accept a price for doing what one is not bound to do. But one who has money is not bound in every case to lend it to his neighbor. Therefore it is lawful for him sometimes to accept a price for lending it.

Obj. 6: Further, silver made into coins does not differ specifically from silver made into a vessel. But it is lawful to accept a price for the loan of a silver vessel. Therefore it is also lawful to accept a price for the loan of a silver coin. Therefore usury is not in itself a sin.

Obj. 7: Further, anyone may lawfully accept a thing which its owner freely gives him. Now he who accepts the loan, freely gives the usury. Therefore he who lends may lawfully take the usury.

On the contrary, it is written (Exod 22:25): "If thou lend money to any of thy people that is poor, that dwelleth with thee, thou shalt not be hard upon them as an extortioner, nor oppress them with usuries."

I answer that, to take usury for money lent is unjust in itself, because this is to sell what does not exist, and this evidently leads to inequality, which is contrary to justice. In order to make this evident, we must observe that there are certain things the use of which consists in their consumption: thus we consume wine when we use it for drink and we consume wheat when we use it for food. Wherefore in such like things the use of the thing must not be reckoned apart from the thing itself, and whoever is granted the use of the thing, is granted the thing itself, and for this reason, to lend things of this kind is to transfer the ownership. Accordingly, if a man wanted to sell wine separately from the use of the wine, he would be selling the same thing twice, or he would be selling what does not exist, wherefore he would evidently commit a sin of injustice. In like manner he commits an injustice who lends wine or wheat, and asks for double payment, viz. one, the return of the thing in equal measure, the other, the price of the use, which is called usury.

On the other hand, there are things the use of which does not consist in their consumption: thus to use a house is to dwell in it, not to destroy it. Wherefore in such things both may be granted: for instance, one man may hand over to another the ownership of his house while reserving to himself the use of it for a time, or vice versa, he may grant the use of the house, while retaining the ownership. For this reason a man may lawfully make a charge for the use of his house, and, besides this, revendicate the house from the person to whom he has granted its use, as happens in renting and letting a house.

Now money, according to the Philosopher (*Ethic.* v, 5; *Polit.* i, 3) was invented chiefly for the purpose of exchange: and consequently the proper and principal use of money is its consumption or alienation whereby it is sunk in exchange. Hence it is by its very nature unlawful to take payment for the use of money lent, which payment is known as usury: and just as a man is bound to restore other ill-gotten goods, so is he bound to restore the money which he has taken in usury.

Reply Obj. 1: In this passage, usury must be taken figuratively for the increase of spiritual goods which God exacts from us, for He wishes us ever to advance in the goods which we receive from Him: and this is for our own profit, not for His.

Reply Obj. 2: The Jews were forbidden to take usury from their brethren, i.e., from other Jews. By this we are given to understand that to take usury from any man is evil simply, because we ought to treat every man as our neighbor and brother, especially in the state of the Gospel, whereto all are called. Hence it is said without any distinction in Ps. 14:5: "He that hath not put out his money to usury," and Ezek. 18:8: "Who hath not taken usury." They were permitted, however, to take usury from foreigners, not as though it were lawful, but in order to avoid a greater evil, lest, to wit, through avarice to which they were prone according to Isa. 56:11, they should take usury from the Jews who were worshippers of God.

Where we find it promised to them as a reward, "Thou shalt fenerate to many nations," etc., fenerating is to be taken in a broad sense for lending, as in Ecclus. 29:10, where we read: "Many have refused to fenerate, not out of wickedness," i.e., they would not lend. Accordingly, the Jews are promised in reward an abundance of wealth, so that they would be able to lend to others.

Reply Obj. 3: Human laws leave certain things unpunished, on account of the condition of those who are imperfect, and who would be deprived of many advantages, if all sins were strictly forbidden and punishments appointed for them. Wherefore human law has permitted usury, not that it looks upon usury as harmonizing with justice, but lest the advantage of many should be hindered. Hence it is that in civil law it is stated that those things according to natural reason and civil law which are consumed by being used, do not admit of usufruct, and that the senate did not (nor could it) appoint a usufruct to such things, but established a quasi-usufruct, namely by permitting usury. Moreover, the Philosopher, led by natural reason, says (*Polit.* i, 3) that to make money by usury is exceedingly unnatural.

Reply Obj. 4: A man is not always bound to lend, and for this reason it is placed among the counsels. Yet it is a matter of precept not to seek profit by lending: although it may be called a matter of counsel in comparison with the maxims of the Pharisees, who deemed some kinds of usury to be lawful, just as love of one's enemies is a matter of counsel. Or again, He speaks here not of the hope of usurious gain, but of the hope which is put in man. For we ought not to lend or do any good deed through hope in man, but only through hope in God.

Reply Obj. 5: He that is not bound to lend may accept repayment for what he has done, but he must not exact more. Now he is repaid according to equality of justice if he is repaid as much as he lent. Wherefore if he exacts more for the usufruct of a thing which has no other use but the consumption of its substance, he exacts a price of something non-existent: and so his exaction is unjust.

Reply Obj. 6: The principal use of a silver vessel is not its consumption, and so one may lawfully sell its use while retaining one's ownership of it. On the other hand the principal use of silver money is sinking it in exchange, so that it is not lawful to sell its use and at the same time expect the restitution of the amount lent. It must be observed, however, that the secondary use of silver vessels may be an exchange, and such use may not be lawfully sold. In like manner there may be some secondary use of silver money; for instance, a man might lend coins for show, or to be used as security. And a man can licitly buy such a use of money.

Reply Obj. 7: He who gives usury does not give it voluntarily simply, but under a certain necessity, insofar as he needs to borrow money which the owner is unwilling to lend without usury.

Article 2: Whether it is lawful to ask for any other kind of consideration for money lent?

Objection 1: It would seem that one may ask for some other kind of consideration for money lent. For everyone may lawfully seek to indemnify himself. Now sometimes a man suffers loss through lending money. Therefore he may lawfully ask for or even exact something else besides the money lent.

Obj. 2: Further, as stated in *Ethic.* v, 5, one is in duty bound by a point of honor, to repay anyone who has done us a favor. Now to lend money to one who is in straits is to do him a favor for which he should be grateful. Therefore the recipient of a loan is bound by a natural debt to repay something. Now it does not seem unlawful to bind oneself to an obligation of the natural law. Therefore it is not unlawful, in lending money to anyone, to demand some sort of compensation as condition of the loan.

Obj. 3: Further, just as there is real remuneration, so is there verbal remuneration, and remuneration by service, as a gloss says on Isa. 33:15, "Blessed is he that shaketh his hands from all bribes." Now it is lawful to accept service or praise from one to whom one has lent money. Therefore in like manner it is lawful to accept any other kind of remuneration.

Obj. 4: Further, seemingly the relation of gift to gift is the same as of loan to loan. But it is lawful to accept money for money given. Therefore it is lawful to accept repayment by loan in return for a loan granted.

Obj. 5: Further, the lender, by transferring his ownership of a sum of money removes the money further from himself than he who entrusts it to a merchant or craftsman. Now it is lawful to receive interest for money entrusted to a merchant or craftsman. Therefore it is also lawful to receive interest for money lent.

Obj. 6: Further, a man may accept a pledge for money lent, the use of which pledge he might sell for a price: as when a man mortgages his land or the house wherein he dwells. Therefore it is lawful to receive interest for money lent.

Obj. 7: Further, it sometimes happens that a man raises the price of his goods under guise of loan, or buys another's goods at a low figure; or raises his price through delay in being paid, and lowers his price that he may be paid the sooner. Now in all these cases there seems to be payment for a loan of money: nor does it appear to be manifestly illicit. Therefore it seems to be lawful to expect or exact some consideration for money lent.

On the contrary, among other conditions requisite in a just man it is stated (Ezek. 18:17) that "he hath not taken usury and increase."

I answer that, according to the Philosopher (*Ethic.* iv, 1), a thing is reckoned as money if its value can be measured by money. Consequently, just as it is a sin against justice, to take money by tacit or express agreement, in return for lending money or anything else that is consumed by being used, so also is it a like sin, by tacit or express agreement to receive anything whose price can be measured by money. Yet there would be no sin in receiving something of the kind, not as exacting it, nor yet as though it were due on account of some agreement tacit or expressed, but as a gratuity: since, even before lending the money, one could accept a gratuity, nor is one in a worse condition through lending.

On the other hand, it is lawful to exact compensation for a loan, in respect of such things as are not appreciated by a measure of money, for instance, benevolence, and love for the lender, and so forth.

Reply Obj. 1: A lender may without sin enter an agreement with the borrower for compensation for the loss he incurs of something he ought to have, for this is not to sell the use of money, but to avoid a loss. It may also happen that the borrower avoids a greater loss than the lender incurs, wherefore the borrower may repay the lender with what he has gained. But the lender cannot enter an agreement for compensation, through the fact that he makes no profit out of his money: because he must not sell that which he has not yet and may be prevented in many ways from having.

Reply Obj. 2: Repayment for a favor may be made in two ways. In one way, as a debt of justice; and to such a debt a man may be bound by a fixed contract; and its amount is measured according to the favor received. Wherefore the borrower of money or any such thing the use of which is its consumption is not bound to repay more than he received in loan: and consequently it is against justice if he be obliged to pay back more. In another way, a man's obligation to repayment for favor received is based on a debt of friendship, and the nature of this debt depends more on the feeling with which the favor was conferred than on the greatness of the favor itself. This debt does not carry with it a civil obligation, involving a kind of necessity that would exclude the spontaneous nature of such a repayment.

Reply Obj. 3: If a man were, in return for money lent, as though there had been an agreement tacit or expressed, to expect or exact repayment in the shape of some remuneration of service or words, it would be the same as if he expected or exacted some real remuneration, because both can be priced at a money value, as may be seen in the case of those who offer for hire the labor which they exercise by work or by tongue. If on the other hand the remuneration by service or words be given not as an obligation, but as a favor, which is not to be appreciated at a money value, it is lawful to take, exact, and expect it.

Reply Obj. 4: Money cannot be sold for a greater sum than the amount lent, which has to be paid back: nor should the loan be made with a demand or expectation of aught else but of a feeling of benevolence which cannot be priced at a pecuniary value, and which can be the basis of a spontaneous loan. Now the obligation to lend in return at some future time is repugnant to such a feeling, because again an obligation of this kind has its pecuniary value. Consequently it is lawful for the lender to borrow something else at the same time, but it is unlawful for him to bind the borrower to grant him a loan at some future time.

Reply Obj. 5: He who lends money transfers the ownership of the money to the borrower. Hence the borrower holds the money at his own risk and is bound to pay it all back: wherefore the lender must not exact more. On the other hand, he that entrusts his money to a merchant or craftsman so as to form a kind of society, does not transfer the ownership of his money to them, for it remains his, so that at his risk the merchant speculates with it, or the craftsman uses it for his craft, and consequently he may lawfully demand as something belonging to him, part of the profits derived from his money.

Reply Obj. 6: If a man in return for money lent to him pledges something that can be valued at a price, the lender must allow for the use of that thing towards the repayment of the loan. Else if he wishes the gratuitous use of that thing in addition to repayment, it is the same as if he took money for lending, and that is usury, unless perhaps it were such a thing as friends are wont to lend to one another gratis, as in the case of the loan of a book.

Reply Obj. 7: If a man wish to sell his goods at a higher price than that which is just, so that he may wait for the buyer to pay, it is manifestly a case of usury: because this waiting for the payment of the price has the character of a loan, so that whatever he demands beyond the just price in consideration of this delay, is like a price for a loan, which pertains to usury. In like manner, if a buyer wishes to buy goods at a lower price than what is just, for the reason that he pays for the goods before they can be delivered, it is a sin of usury; because again this anticipated payment of money has the character of a loan, the price of which is the rebate on the just price of the goods sold. On the other hand, if a man wishes to allow a rebate on the just price in order that he may have his money sooner, he is not guilty of the sin of usury.

Article 3: Whether a man is bound to restore whatever profits he has made out of money gotten by usury?

Objection 1: It would seem that a man is bound to restore whatever profits he has made out of money gotten by usury. For the Apostle says (Rom 11:16): "If the root be holy, so are the branches." Therefore likewise if the root be rotten so are the branches. But the root was infected with usury. Therefore whatever profit is made therefrom is infected with usury. Therefore he is bound to restore it.

Obj. 2: Further, it is laid down (Extra, De Usuris, in the Decretal: Cum tu sicut asseris): "Property accruing from usury must be sold, and the price repaid to the persons from whom the usury was extorted." Therefore, likewise, whatever else is acquired from usurious money must be restored.

Obj. 3: Further, that which a man buys with the proceeds of usury is due to him by reason of the money he paid for it. Therefore he has no more right to the thing purchased than to the money he paid. But he was bound to restore the money gained through usury. Therefore he is also bound to restore what he acquired with it.

On the contrary, A man may lawfully hold what he has lawfully acquired. Now that which is acquired by the proceeds of usury is sometimes lawfully acquired. Therefore it may be lawfully retained.

I answer that, As stated above (A. 1), there are certain things whose use is their consumption, and which do not admit of usufruct, according to law (ibid., ad 3). Wherefore if such like things be extorted by means of usury, for instance money, wheat, wine and so forth, the lender is not bound to restore more than he received (since what is acquired by such things is the fruit not of the thing but of human industry), unless indeed the other party by losing some of his own goods be injured through the lender retaining them: for then he is bound to make good the loss.

On the other hand, there are certain things whose use is not their consumption: such things admit of usufruct, for instance house or land property and so forth. Wherefore if a man has by usury extorted from another his house or land, he is bound to restore not only the house or land but also the fruits accruing to him therefrom, since they are the fruits of things owned by another man and consequently are due to him.

Reply Obj. 1: The root has not only the character of matter, as money made by usury has; but has also somewhat the character of an active cause, insofar as it administers nourishment. Hence the comparison fails.

Reply Obj. 2: Further, property acquired from usury does not belong to the person who paid usury, but to the person who bought it. Yet he that paid usury has a certain claim on that property just as he has on the other goods of the usurer. Hence it is not prescribed that such property should be assigned to the persons who paid usury, since the property is perhaps worth more than what they paid in usury, but it is commanded that the property be sold, and the price be restored, of course according to the amount taken in usury.

Reply Obj. 3: The proceeds of money taken in usury are due to the person who acquired them, not by reason of the usurious money as instrumental cause, but on account of his own industry as principal cause. Wherefore he has more right to the goods acquired with usurious money than to the usurious money itself.

Article 4: Whether it is lawful to borrow money under a condition of usury?

Objection 1: It would seem that it is not lawful to borrow money under a condition of usury. For the Apostle says (Rom 1:32) that "they are worthy of death . . . not only they that do these sins, but they also that consent to them that do them." Now he that borrows money under a condition of usury consents in the sin of the usurer, and gives him an occasion of sin. Therefore he sins also.

Obj. 2: Further, for no temporal advantage ought one to give another an occasion of committing a sin: for this pertains to active scandal, which is always sinful, as stated above (Q. 43, art. 2). Now he that seeks to borrow from a usurer gives him an occasion of sin. Therefore he is not to be excused on account of any temporal advantage.

Obj. 3: Further, it seems no less necessary sometimes to deposit one's money with a usurer than to borrow from him. Now it seems altogether unlawful to deposit one's money with a usurer, even as it would be unlawful to deposit one's sword with a madman, a maiden with a libertine, or food with a glutton. Neither therefore is it lawful to borrow from a usurer.

On the contrary, He that suffers injury does not sin, according to the Philosopher (*Ethic.* v, 11), wherefore justice is not a mean between two vices, as stated in the same book (ch. 5). Now a usurer sins by doing an injury to the person who borrows from him under a condition of usury. Therefore he that accepts a loan under a condition of usury does not sin.

I answer that, It is by no means lawful to induce a man to sin, yet it is lawful to make use of another's sin for a good end, since even God uses all sin for some good, since He draws some good from every evil, as stated in the *Enchiridion* (xi). Hence when Publicola asked whether it were lawful to make use of an oath taken by a man swearing by false gods (which is a manifest sin, for he gives Divine honor to them), Augustine (*Ep.* xlvii) answered that he who uses, not for a bad but for a good purpose, the oath of a man that swears by false gods, is a party, not to his sin of swearing by demons, but to his good compact whereby he kept his word. If however he were to induce him to swear by false gods, he would sin.

Accordingly we must also answer to the question in point that it is by no means lawful to induce a man to lend under a condition of usury: yet it is lawful to borrow for usury from a man who is ready to do so and is a usurer by profession; provided the borrower have a good end in view, such as the relief of his own or another's need. Thus too it is lawful for a man who has fallen among thieves to point out his property to them (which they sin in taking) in order to save his life, after the example of the ten men who said to Ismahel (Jer 41:8): "Kill us not: for we have stores in the field."

Reply Obj. 1: He who borrows for usury does not consent to the usurer's sin but makes use of it. Nor is it the usurer's acceptance of usury that pleases him, but his lending, which is good.

Reply Obj. 2: He who borrows for usury gives the usurer an occasion, not for taking usury, but for lending; it is the usurer who finds an occasion of sin in the malice of his heart. Hence there is passive scandal on his part, while there is no active scandal on the part of the person who seeks to borrow. Nor is this passive scandal a reason why the other person should desist from borrowing if he is in need, since this passive scandal arises not from weakness or ignorance but from malice.

Reply Obj. 3: If one were to entrust one's money to a usurer lacking other means of practising usury; or with the intention of making a greater profit from his money by reason of the usury, one would be giving a sinner matter for sin, so that one would be a participator in his guilt. If, on the other hand, the usurer to whom one entrusts one's money has other means of practising usury, there is no sin in entrusting it to him that it may be in safer keeping, since this is to use a sinner for a good purpose.

QUAESTIO 78: DE PECCATO USURAE

Deinde considerandum est de peccato usurae, quod committitur in mutuis. Et circa hoc quaeruntur quatuor. Primo, utrum sit peccatum accipere pecuniam in pretium pro pecunia mutuata, quod est accipere usuram. Secundo, utrum liceat pro eodem quamcumque utilitatem accipere quasi in recompensationem mutui. Tertio, utrum aliquis restituere teneatur id quod de pecunia usuraria iusto lucro lucratus est. Quarto, utrum liceat accipere mutuo pecuniam sub usura.

Articulus 1: Utrum accipere usuram pro pecunia mutuata sit peccatum

Ad primum sic proceditur. Videtur quod accipere usuram pro pecunia mutuata non sit peccatum. Nullus enim peccat ex hoc quod sequitur exemplum Christi. Sed dominus de seipso dicit, Luc. XIX, ego veniens cum usuris exegissem illam, scilicet pecuniam mutuatam. Ergo non est peccatum accipere usuram pro mutuo pecuniae.

Praeterea, sicut dicitur in Psalm., lex domini immaculata, quia scilicet peccatum prohibet. Sed in lege divina conceditur aliqua usura, secundum illud Deut. XXIII, non faenerabis fratri tuo ad usuram pecuniam, nec fruges nec quamlibet aliam rem, sed alieno. Et, quod plus est, etiam in praemium repromittitur pro lege servata, secundum illud

Deut. XXVIII, faenerabis gentibus multis; et ipse a nullo faenus accipies. Ergo accipere usuram non est peccatum.

Praeterea, in rebus humanis determinatur iustitia per leges civiles. Sed secundum eas conceditur usuras accipere. Ergo videtur non esse illicitum.

Praeterea, praetermittere consilia non obligat ad peccatum. Sed Luc. VI inter alia consilia ponitur, date mutuum, nihil inde sperantes. Ergo accipere usuram non est peccatum.

Praeterea, pretium accipere quo eo quod quis facere non tenetur, non videtur esse secundum se peccatum. Sed non in quolibet casu tenetur pecuniam habens eam proximo mutuare. Ergo licet ei aliquando pro mutuo accipere pretium.

Praeterea, argentum monetatum, et in vasa formatum, non differt specie. Sed licet accipere pretium pro vasis argenteis accommodatis. Ergo etiam licet accipere pretium pro mutuo argenti monetati. Usura ergo non est secundum se peccatum.

Praeterea, quilibet potest licite accipere rem quam ei dominus rei voluntarie tradit. Sed ille qui accipit mutuum voluntarie tradit usuram. Ergo ille qui mutuat licite potest accipere.

Sed contra est quod dicitur Exod. XXII, si pecuniam mutuam dederis populo meo pauperi qui habitat tecum, non urgebis eum quasi exactor, nec usuris opprimes.

Respondeo dicendum quod accipere usuram pro pecunia mutuata est secundum se iniustum, quia venditur id quod non est, per quod manifeste inaequalitas constituitur, quae iustitiae contrariatur. Ad cuius evidentiam, sciendum est quod quaedam res sunt quarum usus est ipsarum rerum consumptio, sicut vinum consumimus eo utendo ad potum, et triticum consumimus eo utendo ad cibum. Unde in talibus non debet seorsum computari usus rei a re ipsa, sed cuicumque conceditur usus, ex hoc ipso conceditur res. Et propter hoc in talibus per mutuum transfertur dominium. Si quis ergo seorsum vellet vendere vinum et seorsum vellet vendere usum vini, venderet eandem rem bis, vel venderet id quod non est. Unde manifeste per iniustitiam peccaret. Et simili ratione, iniustitiam committit qui mutuat vinum aut triticum petens sibi duas recompensationes, unam quidem restitutionem aequalis rei, aliam vero pretium usus, quod usura dicitur.

Quaedam vero sunt quorum usus non est ipsa rei consumptio, sicut usus domus est inhabitatio, non autem dissipatio. Et ideo in talibus seorsum potest utrumque concedi, puta cum aliquis tradit alteri dominium domus, reservato sibi usu ad aliquod tempus; vel e converso cum quis concedit alicui usum domus, reservato sibi eius dominio. Et propter hoc licite potest homo accipere pretium pro usu domus, et praeter hoc petere domum commodatam, sicut patet in conductione et locatione domus.

Pecunia autem, secundum philosophum, in V Ethic. et in I Polit., principaliter est inventa ad commutationes faciendas, et ita proprius et principalis pecuniae usus est ipsius consumptio sive distractio, secundum quod in commutationes expenditur. Et propter hoc secundum se est illicitum pro usu pecuniae mutuatae accipere pretium, quod dicitur usura. Et sicut alia iniuste acquisita tenetur homo restituere, ita pecuniam quam per usuram accepit.

Ad primum ergo dicendum quod usura ibi metaphorice accipitur pro superexcrescentia bonorum spiritualium, quam exigit Deus volens ut in bonis acceptis ab eo semper proficiamus. Quod est ad utilitatem nostram, non eius.

Ad secundum dicendum quod Iudaeis prohibitum fuit accipere usuram a fratribus suis, scilicet Iudaeis, per quod datur intelligi quod accipere usuram a quocumque homine est simpliciter malum; debemus enim omnem hominem habere quasi proximum et fratrem, praecipue in statu Evangelii, ad quod omnes vocantur. Unde in Psalm. absolute dicitur, qui pecuniam suam non dedit ad usuram; et Ezech. XVIII, qui usuram non acceperit. Quod autem ab extraneis usuram acciperent, non fuit eis concessum quasi licitum, sed permissum ad maius malum vitandum, ne scilicet a Iudaeis, Deum colentibus, usuras acciperent, propter avaritiam, cui dediti erant, ut habetur Isaiae LVI.

Quod autem in praemium promittitur, faenerabis gentibus multis, etc., faenus ibi large accipitur pro mutuo, sicut et Eccli. XXIX dicitur, multi non causa nequitiae non faenerati sunt, idest non mutuaverunt. Promittitur ergo in praemium Iudaeis abundantia divitiarum, ex qua contingit quod aliis mutuare possint.

Ad tertium dicendum quod leges humanae dimittunt aliqua peccata impunita propter conditiones hominum imperfectorum, in quibus multae utilitates impedirentur si omnia peccata districte prohiberentur poenis adhibitis. Et ideo usuras lex humana concessit, non quasi existimans eas esse secundum iustitiam, sed ne impedirentur utilitates multorum. Unde in ipso iure civili dicitur quod res quae usu consumuntur neque ratione naturali neque civili recipiunt usumfructum, et quod senatus non fecit earum rerum usumfructum, nec enim poterat; sed quasi usumfructum constituit, concedens scilicet usuras. Et philosophus, naturali ratione ductus, dicit, in I Polit., quod usuraria acquisitio pecuniarum est maxime praeter naturam.

Ad quartum dicendum quod dare mutuum non semper tenetur homo, et ideo quantum ad hoc ponitur inter consilia. Sed quod homo lucrum de mutuo non quaerat, hoc cadit sub ratione praecepti. Potest tamen dici consilium per comparationem ad dicta Pharisaeorum, qui putabant usuram aliquam esse licitam, sicut et dilectio inimicorum est consilium. Vel loquitur ibi non de spe usurarii lucri, sed de spe quae ponitur in homine. Non enim debemus mutuum dare, vel quodcumque bonum facere, propter spem hominis, sed propter spem Dei.

Ad quintum dicendum quod ille qui mutuare non tenetur recompensationem potest accipere eius quod fecit, sed non amplius debet exigere. Recompensatur autem sibi secundum aequalitatem iustitiae si tantum ei reddatur quantum mutuavit. Unde si amplius exigat pro usufructu rei quae alium usum non habet nisi consumptionem substantiae, exigit pretium eius quod non est. Et ita est iniusta exactio.

Ad sextum dicendum quod usus principalis vasorum argenteorum non est ipsa eorum consumptio, et ideo usus eorum potest vendi licite, servato dominio rei. Usus autem principalis pecuniae argenteae est distractio pecuniae in commutationes. Unde non licet eius usum vendere cum hoc quod aliquis velit eius restitutionem quod mutuo dedit. Sciendum tamen quod secundarius usus argenteorum vasorum posset esse commutatio. Et talem usum eorum vendere non liceret. Et similiter potest esse aliquis alius secundarius usus pecuniae argenteae, ut puta si quis concederet pecuniam signatam ad ostentationem, vel ad ponendum loco pignoris. Et talem usum pecuniae licite homo vendere potest.

Ad septimum dicendum quod ille qui dat usuram non simpliciter voluntarie dat, sed cum quadam necessitate, inquantum indiget pecuniam accipere mutuo, quam ille qui habet non vult sine usura mutuare.

Articulus 2: Utrum aliquis possit pro pecunia mutuata aliquam aliam commoditatem expetere

Ad secundum sic proceditur. Videtur quod aliquis possit pro pecunia mutuata aliquam aliam commoditatem expetere. Unusquisque enim licite potest suae indemnitati consulere. Sed quandoque damnum aliquis patitur ex hoc quod pecuniam mutuat. Ergo licitum est ei, supra pecuniam mutuatam, aliquid aliud pro damno expetere, vel etiam exigere.

Praeterea, unusquisque tenetur ex quodam debito honestatis aliquid recompensare ei qui sibi gratiam fecit, ut dicitur in V Ethic. Sed ille qui alicui in necessitate constituto pecuniam mutuat, gratiam facit, unde et gratiarum actio ei debetur. Ergo ille qui recipit tenetur naturali debito aliquid recompensare. Sed non videtur esse illicitum obligare se ad aliquid ad quod quis ex naturali iure tenetur. Ergo non videtur esse illicitum si aliquis, pecuniam alteri mutuans, in obligationem deducat aliquam recompensationem.

Praeterea, sicut est quoddam munus a manu, ita est munus a lingua, et ab obsequio, ut dicit Glossa Isaiae XXXIII, beatus qui excutit manus suas ab omni munere.

Sed licet accipere servitium, vel etiam laudem, ab eo cui quis pecuniam mutuavit. Ergo, pari ratione, licet quodcumque aliud munus accipere.

Praeterea, eadem videtur esse comparatio dati ad datum et mutuati ad mutuatum. Sed licet pecuniam accipere pro alia pecunia data. Ergo licet accipere recompensationem alterius mutui pro pecunia mutuata.

Praeterea, magis a se pecuniam alienat qui, eam mutuando, dominium transfert, quam qui eam mercatori vel artifici committit. Sed licet lucrum accipere de pecunia commissa mercatori vel artifici. Ergo licet etiam lucrum accipere de pecunia mutuata.

Praeterea, pro pecunia mutuata potest homo pignus accipere, cuius usus posset aliquo pretio vendi, sicut cum impignoratur ager vel domus quae inhabitatur. Ergo licet aliquod lucrum habere de pecunia mutuata.

Praeterea, contingit quandoque quod aliquis carius vendit res suas ratione mutui; aut vilius emit quod est alterius; vel etiam pro dilatione pretium auget, vel pro acceleratione diminuit, in quibus omnibus videtur aliqua recompensatio fieri quasi pro mutuo pecuniae. Hoc autem non manifeste apparet illicitum. Ergo videtur licitum esse aliquod commodum de pecunia mutuata expectare, vel etiam exigere.

Sed contra est quod Ezech. XVIII dicitur, inter alia quae ad virum iustum requiruntur, usuram et superabundantiam non acceperit.

Respondeo dicendum quod, secundum philosophum, in IV Ethic., omne illud pro pecunia habetur cuius pretium potest pecunia mensurari. Et ideo sicut si aliquis pro pecunia mutuata, vel quacumque alia re quae ex ipso usu consumitur, pecuniam accipit ex pacto tacito vel expresso, peccat contra iustitiam, ut dictum est; ita etiam quicumque ex pacto tacito vel expresso quodcumque aliud acceperit cuius pretium pecunia mensurari potest, simile peccatum incurrit. Si vero accipiat aliquid huiusmodi non quasi exigens, nec quasi ex aliqua obligatione tacita vel expressa, sed sicut gratuitum donum, non peccat, quia etiam antequam pecuniam mutuasset, licite poterat aliquod donum gratis accipere, nec peioris conditionis efficitur per hoc quod mutuavit.

Recompensationem vero eorum quae pecunia non mensurantur licet pro mutuo exigere, puta benevolentiam et amorem eius qui mutuavit, vel aliquid huiusmodi.

Ad primum ergo dicendum quod ille qui mutuum dat potest absque peccato in pactum deducere cum eo qui mutuum accipit recompensationem damni per quod subtrahitur sibi aliquid quod debet habere, hoc enim non est vendere usum pecuniae, sed damnum vitare. Et potest esse quod accipiens mutuum maius damnum evitet quam dans incurret, unde accipiens mutuum cum sua utilitate damnum alterius recompensat. Recompensationem vero damni quod consideratur in hoc quod de pecunia non lucratur, non potest in pactum deducere, quia non debet vendere id quod nondum habet et potest impediri multipliciter ab habendo.

Ad secundum dicendum quod recompensatio alicuius beneficii dupliciter fieri potest. Uno quidem modo, ex debito iustitiae, ad quod aliquis ex certo pacto obligari potest. Et hoc debitum attenditur secundum quantitatem beneficii quod quis accepit. Et ideo ille qui accipit mutuum pecuniae, vel cuiuscumque similis rei cuius usus est eius consumptio, non tenetur ad plus recompensandum quam mutuo acceperit. Unde contra iustitiam est si ad plus reddendum obligetur. Alio modo tenetur aliquis ad recompensandum beneficium ex debito amicitiae, in quo magis consideratur affectus ex quo aliquis beneficium contulit quam etiam quantitas eius quod fecit. Et tali debito non competit civilis obligatio, per quam inducitur quaedam necessitas, ut non spontanea recompensatio fiat.

Ad tertium dicendum quod si aliquis ex pecunia mutuata expectet vel exigat, quasi per obligationem pacti taciti vel expressi, recompensationem muneris ab obsequio vel lingua, perinde est ac si expectaret vel exigeret munus a manu, quia utrumque pecunia aestimari potest, ut patet in his qui locant operas suas, quas manu vel lingua exercent. Si vero munus ab obsequio vel lingua non quasi ex obligatione rei exhibeat, sed ex benevolentia, quae sub aestimatione pecuniae non cadit, licet hoc accipere et exigere et expectare.

Ad quartum dicendum quod pecunia non potest vendi pro pecunia ampliori quam sit quantitas pecuniae mutuatae, quae restituenda est, nec ibi aliquid est exigendum aut expectandum nisi benevolentiae affectus, qui sub aestimatione pecuniae non cadit, ex quo potest procedere spontanea mutuatio. Repugnat autem ei obligatio ad mutuum in posterum faciendum, quia etiam talis obligatio pecunia aestimari posset. Et ideo licet simul mutuanti unum aliquid aliud mutuare, non autem licet eum obligare ad mutuum in posterum faciendum.

Ad quintum dicendum quod ille qui mutuat pecuniam transfert dominium pecuniae in eum cui mutuat. Unde ille cui pecunia mutuatur sub suo periculo tenet eam, et tenetur integre restituere. Unde non debet amplius exigere ille qui mutuavit. Sed ille qui committit pecuniam suam vel mercatori vel artifici per modum societatis cuiusdam, non transfert dominium pecuniae suae in illum, sed remanet eius, ita quod cum periculo ipsius mercator de ea negotiatur vel artifex operatur. Et ideo licite potest partem lucri inde provenientis expetere, tanquam de re sua.

Ad sextum dicendum quod si quis pro pecunia sibi mutuata obliget rem aliquam cuius usus pretio aestimari potest, debet usum illius rei ille qui mutuavit computare in restitutionem eius quod mutuavit. Alioquin, si usum illius rei quasi gratis sibi superaddi velit, idem est ac si pecuniam acciperet pro mutuo, quod est usurarium, nisi forte esset talis res cuius usus sine pretio soleat concedi inter amicos, sicut patet de libro accommodato.

Ad septimum dicendum quod si aliquis carius velit vendere res suas quam sit iustum pretium, ut de pecunia solvenda emptorem expectet, usura manifeste committitur, quia huiusmodi expectatio pretii solvendi habet rationem mutui; unde quidquid ultra iustum pretium pro huiusmodi expectatione exigitur, est quasi pretium mutui, quod pertinet ad rationem usurae. Similiter etiam si quis emptor velit rem emere vilius quam sit iustum pretium, eo quod pecuniam ante solvit quam possit ei tradi, est peccatum usurae, quia etiam ista anticipatio solutionis pecuniae habet mutui rationem, cuius quoddam pretium est quod diminuitur de iusto pretio rei emptae. Si vero aliquis de iusto pretio velit diminuere ut pecuniam prius habeat, non peccat peccato usurae.

Articulus 3: Utrum quidquid aliquis de pecunia usuraria lucratus fuerit, reddere teneatur

Ad tertium sic proceditur. Videtur quod quidquid aliquis de pecunia usuraria lucratus fuerit, reddere teneatur. Dicit enim apostolus, ad Rom. XI, si radix sancta, et rami. Ergo, eadem ratione, si radix infecta, et rami. Sed radix fuit usuraria. Ergo et quidquid ex ea acquisitum est, est usurarium. Ergo tenetur ad restitutionem illius.

Praeterea, sicut dicitur extra, de usuris, in illa decretali, cum tu sicut asseris, possessiones quae de usuris sunt comparatae debent vendi, et ipsarum pretia his a quibus sunt extorta restitui. Ergo, eadem ratione, quidquid aliud ex pecunia usuraria acquiritur debet restitui.

Praeterea, illud quod aliquis emit de pecunia usuraria debetur sibi ratione pecuniae quam dedit. Non ergo habet maius ius in re quam acquisivit quam in pecunia quam dedit. Sed pecuniam usurariam tenebatur restituere. Ergo et illud quod ex ea acquirit tenetur restituere.

Sed contra, quilibet potest licite tenere id quod legitime acquisivit. Sed id quod acquiritur per pecuniam usurariam interdum legitime acquiritur. Ergo licite potest retineri.

Respondeo dicendum quod, sicut supra dictum est, res quaedam sunt quarum usus est ipsarum rerum consumptio, quae non habent usumfructum, secundum iura. Et ideo si talia fuerint per usuram extorta, puta denarii, triticum, vinum aut aliquid huiusmodi, non tenetur homo ad restituendum nisi id quod accepit, quia id quod de tali re est acquisitum non est fructus huius rei, sed humanae industriae. Nisi forte per detentionem talis rei alter sit damnificatus, amittendo aliquid de bonis suis, tunc enim tenetur ad recompensationem nocumenti.

Quaedam vero res sunt quarum usus non est earum consumptio, et talia habent usumfructum, sicut domus et ager et alia huiusmodi. Et ideo si quis domum alterius vel agrum per usuram extorsisset, non solum teneretur restituere domum vel agrum, sed etiam fructus inde perceptos, quia sunt fructus rerum quarum alius est dominus, et ideo ei debentur.

Ad primum ergo dicendum quod radix non solum habet rationem materiae, sicut pecunia usuraria, sed habet etiam aliqualiter rationem causae activae, inquantum administrat nutrimentum. Et ideo non est simile.

Ad secundum dicendum quod possessiones quae de usuris sunt comparatae non sunt eorum quorum fuerunt usurae, sed illorum qui eas emerunt. Sunt tamen obligatae illis a quibus fuerunt usurae acceptae, sicut et alia bona usurarii. Et ideo non praecipitur quod assignentur illae possessiones his a quibus fuerunt acceptae usurae, quia forte plus valent quam usurae quas dederunt, sed praecipitur quod vendantur possessiones et earum pretia restituantur, scilicet secundum quantitatem usurae acceptae.

Ad tertium dicendum quod illud quod acquiritur de pecunia usuraria debetur quidem acquirenti propter pecuniam usurariam datam sicut propter causam instrumentalem, sed propter suam industriam sicut propter causam principalem. Et ideo plus iuris habet in re acquisita de pecunia usuraria quam in ipsa pecunia usuraria.

Articulus 4: Utrum liceat pecuniam accipere mutuo sub usura

Ad quartum sic proceditur. Videtur quod non liceat pecuniam accipere mutuo sub usura. Dicit enim apostolus, Rom. I, quod digni sunt morte non solum qui faciunt peccata, sed etiam qui consentiunt facientibus. Sed ille qui accipit pecuniam mutuo sub usuris consentit usurario in suo peccato, et praebet ei occasionem peccandi. Ergo etiam ipse peccat.

Appendices

Praeterea, pro nullo commodo temporali debet aliquis alteri quamcumque occasionem praebere peccandi, hoc enim pertinet ad rationem scandali activi, quod semper est peccatum, ut supra dictum est. Sed ille qui petit mutuum ab usurario expresse dat ei occasionem peccandi. Ergo pro nullo commodo temporali excusatur.

Praeterea, non minor videtur esse necessitas quandoque deponendi pecuniam suam apud usurarium quam mutuum accipiendi ab ipso. Sed deponere pecuniam apud usurarium videtur esse omnino illicitum, sicut illicitum esset deponere gladium apud furiosum, vel virginem committere luxurioso, seu cibum guloso. Ergo neque licitum est accipere mutuum ab usurario.

Sed contra, ille qui iniuriam patitur non peccat, secundum philosophum, in V Ethic., unde iustitia non est media inter duo vitia, ut ibidem dicitur. Sed usurarius peccat inquantum facit iniustitiam accipienti mutuum sub usuris. Ergo ille qui accipit mutuum sub usuris non peccat.

Respondeo dicendum quod inducere hominem ad peccandum nullo modo licet, uti tamen peccato alterius ad bonum licitum est, quia et Deus utitur omnibus peccatis ad aliquod bonum, ex quolibet enim malo elicit aliquod bonum, ut dicitur in Enchiridio. Et ideo Augustinus Publicolae quaerenti utrum liceret uti iuramento eius qui per falsos deos iurat, in quo manifeste peccat eis reverentiam divinam adhibens, respondit quod qui utitur fide illius qui per falsos deos iurat, non ad malum sed ad bonum, non peccato illius se sociat, quo per Daemonia iuravit, sed pacto bono eius, quo fidem servavit. Si tamen induceret eum ad iurandum per falsos deos, peccaret.

Ita etiam in proposito dicendum est quod nullo modo licet inducere aliquem ad mutuandum sub usuris, licet tamen ab eo qui hoc paratus est facere et usuras exercet, mutuum accipere sub usuris, propter aliquod bonum, quod est subventio suae necessitatis vel alterius. Sicut etiam licet ei qui incidit in latrones manifestare bona quae habet, quae latrones diripiendo peccant, ad hoc quod non occidatur, exemplo decem virorum qui dixerunt ad Ismahel, noli occidere nos, quia habemus thesaurum in agro, ut dicitur Ierem. XLI.

Ad primum ergo dicendum quod ille qui accipit pecuniam mutuo sub usuris non consentit in peccatum usurarii, sed utitur eo. Nec placet ei usurarum acceptio, sed mutuatio, quae est bona.

Ad secundum dicendum quod ille qui accipit pecuniam mutuo sub usuris non dat usurario occasionem usuras accipiendi, sed mutuandi, ipse autem usurarius sumit occasionem peccandi ex malitia cordis sui. Unde scandalum passivum est ex parte sua, non autem activum ex parte petentis mutuum. Nec tamen propter huiusmodi scandalum passivum debet alius a mutuo petendo desistere, si indigeat, quia huiusmodi passivum scandalum non provenit ex infirmitate vel ignorantia, sed ex malitia.

Ad tertium dicendum quod si quis committeret pecuniam suam usurario non habenti alias unde usuras exerceret; vel hac intentione committeret ut inde copiosius per usuram lucraretur; daret materiam peccanti. Unde et ipse esset particeps culpae. Si autem aliquis usurario alias habenti unde usuras exerceat, pecuniam suam committat ut tutius servetur, non peccat, sed utitur homine peccatore ad bonum.

3
DECREES OF THE COUNCIL OF VIENNE

29. Serious suggestions have been made to us that communities in certain places, to the divine displeasure and injury of the neighbour, in violation of both divine and human law, approve of usury. By their statutes, sometimes confirmed by oath, they not only grant that usury may be demanded and paid, but deliberately compel debtors to pay it. By these statutes they impose heavy burdens on those claiming the return of usurious payments, employing also various pretexts and ingenious frauds to hinder the return. We, therefore, wishing to get rid of these pernicious practices, decree with the approval of the sacred council that all the magistrates, captains, rulers, consuls, judges, counsellors, or any other officials of these communities who presume in the future to make, write or dictate such statutes, or knowingly decide that usury be paid or, if paid, that it be not fully and freely restored when claimed, incur the sentence of excommunication. They shall also incur the same sentence unless within three months they delete from the books of their communities, if they have the power, statutes of this kind hitherto published, or if they presume to observe in any way these statutes or customs. Furthermore, since money-lenders for the most part enter into usurious contracts so frequently with secrecy and guile that they can be convicted only with difficulty, we decree that they be compelled by ecclesiastical censure to open their account books, when there is question of usury. If indeed someone has fallen into the error of presuming to affirm pertinaciously that the practice of usury is not sinful, we decree that he is to be punished as a heretic; and we strictly enjoin on local ordinaries and inquisitors of heresy to proceed against those they find suspect of such error as they would against those suspected of heresy.[3]

---

[3] Tanner, *Decrees of the Ecumenical Councils*, vol. I, 384.

29. Ex gravi ad nos insinuatione pervenit, quod quorundam communitates locorum in offensam Dei et proximi ac contra iura divina pariter et humana usurariam approbantes quodammodo pravitatem, per statuta sua iuramento quandoque firmata usuras exigi et solvi nedum concedunt, sed ad solvendas eas debitores scienter compellunt, ac iuxta ipsorum continentiam statutorum gravia imponendo, plerumque usuras repetentibus onera, aliisque utendo super his diversis coloribus et fraudibus exquisitis, repetitionem impediunt earundem. Nos igitur, perniciosis his ausibus obviare volentes, sacro approbante concilio statuimus ut, quicunque communitatum ipsarum potestates, capitanei, rectores, consules, iudices, consiliarii aut alii quivis officiales statuta huiusmodi de cetero facere, scribere vel dictare, aut quod solvantur usurae vel quod solutae, cum repetuntur, non restituantur plene ac libere, scienter iudicare praesumpserint, sententiam excommunicationis incurrant, eandem etiam sententiam incursuri, nisi statuta huiusmodi hactenus edita de libris communitatum ipsarum, si super hoc potestatem habuerint, infra tres menses deleverint, aut si ipsa statuta sive consuetudines, effectum eorum habentes, quoquo modo praesumpserint observare. Ceterum quia feneratores sic ut plurimum contractus usurarios occulte ineunt et dolose, quod vix convinci possunt de usuraria pravitate, ad exhibendum, cum de usuris agetur, suarum codices rationum censura ipsos decernimus ecclesiastica compellendos. Sane si quis in illum errorem inciderit, ut pertinaciter affirmare praesumat, exercere usuras non esse peccatum, decernimus cum velut haereticum puniendum, locorum nihilominus ordinariis et haereticae pravitatis inquisitoribus districtius iniungentes, ut contra eos, quos de errore huiusmodi diffamatos invenerint aut suspectos, tanquam contra diffamatos vel suspectos de haeresi procedere non omittant.

4
REGIMINI UNIVERSALIS
Callistus III, 1455–1458
Usury and Contract for Rent[4]

A PETITION recently addressed to us proposed the following matter: For a very long time, and with nothing in memory running to the contrary, in various parts of Germany, for the common advantage of society, there has been implanted among the inhabitants of those parts and maintained up to this time through constant observance, a certain custom. By this custom, these inhabitants—or, at least, those among them, who in the light of their condition and indemnities, seemed likely to profit from the arrangement—encumber their goods, their houses, their fields, their farms, their possessions, and inheritances, selling the revenues or annual rents in marks, florins, or groats (according as this or that coin is current in those particular regions), and for each mark, florin, or groat in question, from those who have bought those coins, whether as revenues or as rents, have been in the habit of receiving a certain price appropriately fixed as to size according to the character of the particular circumstances, in conformity with the agreements made in respect of the relevant properties between themselves and the buyers. As guarantee for the payment of the aforesaid revenues and rents, they mortgage those of the aforesaid houses, lands, fields, farms, possessions, and inheritances that have been expressly named in the relevant contracts. In the favor of the sellers it is added to the contract that in proportion as they have, in whole or in part, returned to the said buyers the money thus received, they are entirely quit and free of the obligation to pay the revenues and rents corresponding to the sum returned. But

---

[4] From the Constitution *Regimini Universalis*, May 6, 1455. Denzinger, *The Sources of Catholic Dogma*, 231, no. 716.

the buyers, on the other hand, even though the said goods, houses, lands, fields, possessions, and inheritances might by the passage of time be reduced to utter destruction and desolation, would not be empowered to recover even in respect of the price paid.

Now, by some a certain doubt and hesitation is entertained as to whether contracts of this kind are to be considered licit. Consequently, certain debtors, pretending these contracts would be usurious, seek to find thereby an occasion for the nonpayment of revenues and rents owed by them in this way.... We, therefore, ... in order to remove every doubt springing from these hesitations, by our Apostolic authority, do declare by these present letters that the aforesaid contracts are licit and in agreement with law, and that the said sellers, yielding all opposition, are effectively bound to the payment of the rents and revenues in conformity with the terms of the said contracts.

5
INTER MULTIPLICES
Leo X, 1513–1521
"Mountains of Piety" and Usury

WITH the approval of the holy Council, we declare and define that the aforesaid "Mountains of Piety" established by the civil authorities and thus far approved and confirmed by the authority of the Apostolic See, in which a moderate rate of interest is received exclusively for the expenses of the officials and for other things pertaining to their keeping, as is set forth, for an indemnity of these as far as this matter is concerned, beyond the capital without a profit for these same Mountains, neither offer any species of evil, nor furnish an incentive to sin, nor in any way are condemned; nay, rather, that such a loan is worthwhile and is to be praised and approved, and least of all to be considered usury.... Moreover, we declare that all religious and ecclesiastics as well as secular persons, who henceforth shall dare to preach or dispute in word or in writing against the form of the present declaration and sanction, incur the penalty of excommunication of a sentence [automatically] imposed [*latae sententiae*], a privilege of any nature whatsoever notwithstanding.[5]

---

[5] From the Bull *Inter Multiplices*, April 28, 1515. Denzinger, 238, no. 739.

6

CUM ONUS
Pius V, 1566–1572
Given at Rome, 14 Calen. Feb. 1568

WHEREAS at undertaking the burden of the Apostolical servitude we have learned that innumerable contracts of rent have been, and are daily, celebrated, which are not only not confirmed within the limits prescribed by our ancestors for these contracts, but even, what is worse, under conditions directly contrary; moreover, they carry, on the face of them, an ardent stimulus for avarice, a manifest contempt even of the Divine laws, consulting, as we are bound to do, for the salvation of souls and in compliance even with the petitions of pious minds, to remedy by a salutary antidote such grievous disease and pestiferous poisons.

We by this our constitution decree, that rent or an annuity, can by no means be created, or constituted, unless in an immovable thing, or a thing that may be considered as immovable, of its own nature fruitful, and that may be nominally designated by certain limits.

Again, unless in money truly paid down, in the presence of witnesses and a notary, and in the actual celebration of an instrument, but not when the entire and just price is not first received.

We forbid that the payments which are commonly called *anticipated*, be made or brought into agreement.

It is our will that the conventions binding directly or indirectly to the causal accidences the man who is not otherwise liable to them from the nature of the contracts, be by no means valid.

Nor the pact, likewise, taking away or restraining the liberty of alienating the thing subject to the rent, because we wish that thing be always alienated both freely and without the payment of a fine, or a portion of the sales, or of another quantity or thing, as well during the people's life as in their last will.

But, when the thing is to be sold, we wish that the lord of the rent be preferred to all others, and that the conditions of the sale be intimated to him, and that he be waited for a month.

Let the pacts providing that the remiss debtor of the rent be liable to pay the loss, expenses, or salaries of the creditor, to lose the thing, or any part of the thing, subject to the rent, or to forfeit any right arising to him from that contract, or otherwise, or to incur any penalty, be entirely null and void.

Moreover, we strictly forbid both that the rent be augmented, and new rent created upon the same or another thing, in favour of the same, or of a person appointed by him, in consideration of the rents of the past or future time.

And also, we annul the agreements, providing that the payment of the expenses do appertain to the man to whom they do not otherwise, from law and from the nature of the contract, appertain.

Finally, we wish that all rents to be hereafter created, do perish in proportion, not only when the thing is perished in the whole or in part, or rendered in whole or in part fruitless; but that they can be extinguished for the same price, notwithstanding the prescription even of a very long time, even immemorial, nay, of a hundred and more years, notwithstanding any pacts taking away, directly or indirectly, such liberty, with whatever words or clauses they be made up.

But when the income is to be extinguished by delivering the price, we wish that this be intimated two months beforehand, by the person to whom the price ought to be delivered; and that, subsequent to the notice, the price can be recovered, however, within a year, from him, even against his will: and when he is not willing to demand the price within the year, we wish, however, that the rent can be extinguished at any time — the notice, however, being given, as said before, and notwithstanding the things that are mentioned above; and we command that the same course be observed, even when the notice had been often and often given, and the effect never produced.

We also strictly prohibit the pacts, providing the price of the rent be, beyond the case mentioned, recovered from the unwilling man, either for a penalty, or for another cause.

And we judge that contracts to be celebrated hereafter, under any other form, are usurious.

And, notwithstanding, whatever thing should happen, against our orders, to be explicitly or implicitly given, remitted, or forgiven, we wish that it be claimed by the public treasury. We wish that this wholesome decree be observed perpetually, and in every respect, not only in annuities to be newly created, but likewise in alienating them that are at any time already created, provided they be created subsequent to the publication of this decree.

Declaring that the price once affixed to the rent can never be diminished or augmented on account of the quality of the time, or of the contracting parties, or of any other accidence, nor with regard to any persons that may be ultimately concerned.

And though we do not extend this law to the contracts already celebrated, however we do exhort in the Lord all those persons to whom rents have come under another form, to submit each contract to the scrutiny of good religious persons, and to consult the salvation of their own souls.[6]

---

[6] O'Callaghan, *Usury*, 83–85.

7
VARIOUS ERRORS ON MORAL SUBJECTS
Condemned in a decree of the
Holy Office, March 4, 1679
Innocent XI, 1676–1689

SINCE ready cash is more valuable than that to be paid, and since there is no one who does not consider ready cash of greater worth than future cash, a creditor can demand something beyond the principal from the borrower, and for this reason be excused from usury.[7]

---

[7] Denzinger, *The Sources of Catholic Dogma*, 327, no. 1191.

8

VIX PERVENIT
On Usury and Other Dishonest Profits
November 1, 1745
Benedict XIV, 1740–1758

To the Venerable Brothers, Patriarchs, Archbishops, Bishops and Ordinary Clergy of Italy.

Venerable Brothers, Greetings and Apostolic Benediction.

Hardly had the new controversy (namely, whether certain contracts should be held valid) come to our attention, when several opinions began spreading in Italy that hardly seemed to agree with sound doctrine; We decided that We must remedy this. If We did not do so immediately, such an evil might acquire new force by delay and silence. If we neglected our duty, it might even spread further, shaking those cities of Italy so far not affected.

Therefore, We decided to consult with a number of the Cardinals of the Holy Roman Church, who are renowned for their knowledge and competence in theology and canon law. We also called upon many from the regular clergy who were outstanding in both the faculty of theology and that of canon law. We chose some monks, some mendicants, and finally some from the regular clergy. As presiding officer, We appointed one with degrees in both canon and civil law, who had lengthy court experience. We chose the past July 4 for the meeting at which We explained the nature of the whole business. We learned that all had known and considered it already.

2. We then ordered them to consider carefully all aspects of the matter, meanwhile searching for a solution; after this consideration, they were to write out their conclusions. We did not ask them to pass judgment on the contract which gave rise to the controversy since the many documents they would need were not available. Rather We asked that

they establish a fixed teaching on usury, since the opinions recently spread abroad seemed to contradict the Church's doctrine. All complied with these orders. They gave their opinions publicly in two convocations, the first of which was held in our presence last July 18, the other last August 1; then they submitted their opinions in writing to the secretary of the convocation.

3. Indeed they proved to be of one mind in their opinions.

I. The nature of the sin called usury has its proper place and origin in a loan contract. This financial contract between consenting parties demands, by its very nature, that one return to another only as much as he has received. The sin rests on the fact that sometimes the creditor desires more than he has given. Therefore he contends some gain is owed him beyond that which he loaned, but any gain which exceeds the amount he gave is illicit and usurious.

II. One cannot condone the sin of usury by arguing that the gain is not great or excessive, but rather moderate or small; neither can it be condoned by arguing that the borrower is rich; nor even by arguing that the money borrowed is not left idle, but is spent usefully, either to increase one's fortune, to purchase new estates, or to engage in business transactions. The law governing loans consists necessarily in the equality of what is given and returned; once the equality has been established, whoever demands more than that violates the terms of the loan. Therefore if one receives interest, he must make restitution according to the commutative bond of justice; its function in human contracts is to assure equality for each one. This law is to be observed in a holy manner. If not observed exactly, reparation must be made.

III. By these remarks, however, We do not deny that at times together with the loan contract certain other titles — which are not at all intrinsic to the contract — may run parallel with it. From these other titles, entirely just and legitimate reasons arise to demand something over and above the amount due on the contract. Nor is it denied that it is very often possible for someone, by means of contracts differing entirely from loans, to spend and invest money legitimately either to provide oneself with an annual income or to engage in legitimate trade and business. From these types of contracts honest gain may be made.

IV. There are many different contracts of this kind. In these contracts, if equality is not maintained, whatever is received over and above what is fair is a real injustice. Even though it may not fall under the precise rubric of usury (since all reciprocity, both open and hidden, is absent), restitution is obligated. Thus, if everything is done correctly and weighed in the scales of justice, these same legitimate contracts suffice to provide a standard and a principle for engaging in commerce and fruitful business for the common good. Christian minds should not think that gainful commerce can flourish by usuries or other similar injustices. On the contrary, We learn from divine Revelation that justice raises up nations; sin, however, makes nations miserable.

V. But you must diligently consider this, that some will falsely and rashly persuade themselves—and such people can be found anywhere—that together with loan contracts there are other legitimate titles or, excepting loan contracts, they might convince themselves that other just contracts exist, for which it is permissible to receive a moderate amount of interest. Should any one think like this, he will oppose not only the judgment of the Catholic Church on usury, but also common human sense and natural reason. Everyone knows that man is obliged in many instances to help his fellows with a simple, plain loan. Christ Himself teaches this: "Do not refuse to lend to him who asks you." In many circumstances, no other true and just contract may be possible except for a loan. Whoever therefore wishes to follow his conscience must first diligently inquire if, along with the loan, another category exists by means of which the gain he seeks may be lawfully attained.

4. This is how the Cardinals and theologians and the men most conversant with the canons, whose advice We

had asked for in this most serious business, explained their opinions. Also We devoted our private study to this matter before the congregations were convened, while they were in session, and again after they had been held; for We read the opinions of these outstanding men most diligently. Because of this, We approve and confirm whatever is contained in the opinions above, since the professors of Canon Law and Theology, scriptural evidence, the decrees of previous popes, and the authority of Church councils and the Fathers all seem to enjoin it. Besides, We certainly know the authors who hold the opposite opinions and also those who either support and defend those authors or at least who seem to give them consideration. We are also aware that the theologians of regions neighboring those in which the controversy had its origin undertook the defense of the truth with wisdom and seriousness.

5. Therefore, We address these encyclical letters to all Italian Archbishops, Bishops, and priests to make all of you aware of these matters. Whenever Synods are held or sermons preached or instructions on sacred doctrine given, the above opinions must be strictly adhered to. Take great care that no one in your dioceses dares to write or preach the contrary; however, if anyone should refuse to obey, he should be subjected to the penalties imposed by the sacred canons on those who violate Apostolic mandates.

6. Concerning the specific contract which caused these new controversies, We decide nothing for the present; We also shall not decide now about the other contracts in which the theologians and canonists lack agreement. Rekindle your zeal for piety and your conscientiousness so that you may execute what We have given.

7. First of all, show your people with persuasive words that the sin and vice of usury is most emphatically condemned in the Sacred Scriptures; that it assumes various forms and appearances in order that the faithful, restored to liberty and grace by the blood of Christ, may again be driven headlong into ruin. Therefore, if they desire to

invest their money, let them exercise diligent care lest they be snatched by cupidity, the source of all evil; to this end, let them be guided by those who excel in doctrine and the glory of virtue.

8. In the second place, some trust in their own strength and knowledge to such an extent that they do not hesitate to give answers to those questions which demand considerable knowledge of sacred theology and of the canons. But it is essential for these people, also, to avoid extremes, which are always evil. For instance, there are some who judge these matters with such severity that they hold any profit derived from money to be illegal and usurious; in contrast to them, there are some so indulgent and so remiss that they hold any gain whatsoever to be free of usury. Let them not adhere too much to their private opinions. Before they give their answer, let them consult a number of eminent writers; then let them accept those views which they understand to be confirmed by knowledge and authority. And if a dispute should arise, when some contract is discussed, let no insults be hurled at those who hold the contrary opinion; nor let it be asserted that it must be severely censured, particularly if it does not lack the support of reason and of men of reputation. Indeed, clamorous outcries and accusations break the chain of Christian love and give offense and scandal to the people.

9. In the third place, those who desire to keep themselves free and untouched by the contamination of usury and to give their money to another in such a manner that they may receive only legitimate gain should be admonished to make a contract beforehand. In the contract, they should explain the conditions and what gain they expect from their money. This will not only greatly help to avoid concern and anxiety, but will also confirm the contract in the realm of public business. This approach also closes the door on controversies—which have arisen more than once—since it clarifies whether the money, which has been loaned without apparent interest, may actually contain concealed usury.

10. In the fourth place, We exhort you not to listen to those who say that today the issue of usury is present in name only, since gain is almost always obtained from money given to another. How false is this opinion and how far removed from the truth! We can easily understand this if we consider that the nature of one contract differs from the nature of another. By the same token, the things which result from these contracts will differ in accordance with the varying nature of the contracts. Truly an obvious difference exists between gain which arises from money legally, and therefore can be upheld in the courts of both civil and canon law, and gain which is illicitly obtained, and must therefore be returned according to the judgments of both courts. Thus, it is clearly invalid to suggest, on the grounds that some gain is usually received from money lent out, that the issue of usury is irrelevant in our times.

11. These are the chief things We wanted to say to you. We hope that you may command your faithful to observe what these letters prescribe; and that you may undertake effective remedies if disturbances should be stirred up among your people because of this new controversy over usury or if the simplicity and purity of doctrine should become corrupted in Italy. Finally, to you and to the flock committed to your care, We impart the Apostolic Benediction.

Given in Rome at St. Mary Major, November 1, 1745, the sixth year of Our Pontificate.[8]

---

[8] Benedict XIV, *Vix Pervenit*.

BIBLIOGRAPHY

WORKS CITED

Andries, Alin Marius, Anca Copaciu, Radu Popa, and Razvan Vlahu. "Recourse and (Strategic) Mortgage Defaults: Evidence from Changes in Housing Market Laws." *DNB Working Paper*, DeNederlandscheBank, no. 727 (October 2021).

Aquinas, Thomas. *Commentary on the Sentences, Book III, Distinctions 23–60 (Latin-English Opera Omnia)*. Translated by Chris Decaen and Beth Mortensen. The Aquinas Institute for the Study of Sacred Doctrine, Forthcoming.

———. *On Evil*. Translated by Richard Regan. New York: Oxford University Press, 2003.

———. *Summa Theologiae: Secunda Secundae, 1–91*. Translated by Fr. Laurence Shapcote, O.P. Lander, Wyoming: The Aquinas Institute for the Study of Sacred Doctrine, 2012.

Aristotle. *Politics*. Translated by H Rackham. Vol. 21. 23 vols. Loeb Classical Library. London; Cambridge: Heinemann; Harvard University Press, 1944.

Armstrong, Lawrin D. *The Idea of a Moral Economy: Gerard of Siena on Usury, Restitution, and Prescription*. Toronto: Toronto University Press, 2016.

Ashley, W.J. *An Introduction to English Economic History and Theory: The End of the Middle Ages, Pt. 2*. London: Longmans, Green & Co., 1894.

Belloc, Hilaire. *Economics for Helen*. [n.p.]: St. George Educational Trust, 1999.

Benedict XIV. *Vix Pervenit*, 1745. www.papalencyclicals.net/ben14/b14vixpe.htm.

Bentham, Jeremy. *Defence of Usury*. Gloucester: Dodo Press, 2008.

Blake, David. *Financial Market Analysis*. Chichester: Wiley, 2006.

Böhm-Bawerk, Eugen von. *Capital and Interest: A Critical History of Economic Theory*. London; New York: Macmillan and Co., 1890.

———. *The Positive Theory of Capital*. New York: G E Stechert & Co., 1930.

Cannan, Edwin, B.P. Adarkar, B.K. Sandwell, J.M. Keynes, and K.E. Boulding. "Saving and Usury: A Symposium." *The Economic Journal* 42, no. 165 (1932): 123–41.

Cleary, Patrick. *The Church and Usury: An Essay on Some Historical and Theological Aspects of Money Lending*. 1972. Reprint, Hawthorne, California: Christian Book Club of America, 1984.

Coleridge, Henry James. *The Life and Letters of St. Francis Xavier*. Vol. II. Quarterly Series, Fourth. London: Burns and Oates, 1872.

Convention (III) relative to the Treatment of Prisoners of War. (Geneva), 6 U.S.T. 3316; 75 U.N.T.S. 135 § (1949).

Coyne, Edward J. "Mr. Belloc on Usury." *Studies: An Irish Quarterly Review* 21, no. 82 (1932): 283–97.

Decock, Wim. "Knowing before Judging. Law and Economic Analysis in Early Modern Jesuit Ethics." *Journal of Markets and Morality* 21 (2018): 309–30.

Dempsey, Bernard W. *Interest and Usury*. London: Dobson, 1948.

Denzinger, Henry. *The Sources of Catholic Dogma*. Translated by Roy Deferrari. Fitzwilliam, NH: Loreto Publications, 2002.

Dickson T., ed. *Usury: Frequently Asked Questions*. 3rd ed. Saint Paul: Zippy, 2017.

Elliot, Calvin. *Usury: A Scriptural, Ethical and Economic View*. [n.p]: Aeterna Publishing, 2010.

Fagothey, Austin. *Right and Reason: Ethics in Theory and Practice*. 4th ed. St. Louis: C.V. Mosby, 1967.

Farrell, Walter. *A Companion of the Summa*. 3rd ed. New York: Sheed and Ward, 1940.

Faure, Alexander Pierre. "Interest Rates 3: Composition of Interest Rates." *SSRN Electronic Journal*, 23 December 2014.

Fernandez, Anthony M., Levi A. Russell, and Anthony M. Gentile. "Usury and Interest: Correcting Modern Errors." Leonine Institute for Catholic Social Teaching, 22 July 2020. https://leoinstitute.org/policy-papers/.

Feser, Edward. "Classical Natural Law Theory, Property Rights, and Taxation." *Social Philosophy and Policy* 27, no. 1 (2010): 21–52.

Fisher, Irving. *The Theory of Interest: As Determined by Impatience to Spend Income and Opportunity to Invest It*. Mansfield Centre, CT: Martino Publishing, 2012.

Fox, James J. "Slavery, Ethical Aspect Of." In *The Catholic Encyclopaedia: An International Work of Reference on the Constitution, Doctrine, Discipline, and History of the Catholic Church*, 14:39–41. New York: The Encyclopedia Press, 1913.

Hadas, Edward. *Human Goods, Economic Evils: A Moral Approach to the Dismal Science*. Wilmington, Delaware: ISI Books, 2007.

Hayes, M.G. "Keynes's Liquidity Preference and the Usury Doctrine: Their Connection and Continuing Policy Relevance." *Review of Social Economy* 75, no. 4 (2017): 400–416.

Hellie, Richard. "Slavery." In *Encyclopaedia Britannica*, August 2020. www.britannica.com/topic/slavery-sociology.

Helmolz, R.H. "Usury and the Medieval English Church Courts." *Speculum* 61, no. 2 (1986): 364–80.

Hirschfeld, Mary L. *Aquinas and the Market: Toward a Humane Economy*. Cambridge, Massachusetts: Harvard University Press, 2018.

Justinian. *Imperatoris Iustiniani Institutionum, Libri Quattuor*. Edited by Moyle, J. B. 4th ed. Oxford: Clarendon Press, 1903.

———. *The Institutes of Justinian*. Edited by Moyle, J. B. 4th ed. Oxford: Clarendon Press, 1913.

Keynes, John Maynard. *Essays in Persuasion*. New York: W.W. Norton & Co, 1963.

———. *The General Theory of Employment, Interest and Money*. Hertfordshire: Wordsworth Editions Ltd., 2017.

Labat, Alyssa, and Walter Block. "Money Does Not Grow on Trees: An Argument for Usury." *Journal of Business Ethics* 106, no. 3 (2012): 383–87.

Langholm, Odd. *The Aristotelian Analysis of Usury*. Bergen: Universitetsforlaget, 1984.

Lessius, Leonardus. *On Sale, Securities, and Insurance*. Translated by Wim Decock and Nicholas De Sutter. Grand Rapids (Mich.): CLP Academic, 2016.

Lopez, Robert S. *The Commercial Revolution of the Middle Ages, 950–1350*. Cambridge: Cambridge University Press, 1977.

McCall, Brian M. *The Church and the Usurers: Unprofitable Lending for the Modern Economy*. [n.p.]: Sapientia Press of Ave Maria University, 2013.

Medaille, John C. *Toward a Truly Free Market*. Newburyport: Intercollegiate Studies Institute, 2014.

Mill, John Stuart. *Principles of Political Economy: With Some of Their Applications to Social Philosophy*. London: Longmans, Green and Co., 1936.

Mills, Paul S. "Interest in Interest: The Old Testament Ban on Interest and Its Implications for Today." Doctoral thesis, Cambridge University, 1989.

Mueller, John D. *Redeeming Economics: Rediscovering the Missing Element*. Wilmington, DE: ISI Books, 2014.

Munro, John H. "The Medieval Origins of the Financial Revolution: Usury, *Rentes*, and Negotiability." *The International History Review* 25, no. 3 (2003): 505–62.

Noonan, John T. "Development in Moral Doctrine." *Theological Studies* 54 (1993): 662–77.

———. *The Scholastic Analysis of Usury*. Cambridge, MA: Harvard University Press, 1957.

North, Gary. *An Introduction to Christian Economics*. Nutley, N.J.: The Craig Press, 1973.

O'Callaghan, Jeremiah. *Usury; or, Lending at Interest; Also, The Exaction and Payment of Certain Church-Fees, Such as Pew-Rents, Burial-Fees, and the like, Together with Forestalling Traffick;* London: William Cobbett, 1828.

Panzer, Joel S. *The Popes and Slavery*. New York: Alba House, 1996.

Parsons, Anscar. "Economic Significance of the 'Montes Pietatis.'" *Franciscan Studies* 1, no. 3 (1941): 3–28.

Persky, Joseph. "Retrospectives: From Usury to Interest." *The Journal of Economic Perspectives* 21, no. 1 (2007): 227–36.

Polanyi, Karl. *The Great Transformation: The Political and Economic Origins of Our Times*. Boston, MA: Beacon Press, 2001.

Roover, Raymond de. *San Bernardino of Siena and Saint Antonino of Florence: The Two Great Economic Thinkers of the Middle Ages*. The Kress Library of Business and Economics 19. Boston: Baker Library, 1967.

———. "Scholastic Economics: Survival and Lasting Influence from the Sixteenth Century to Adam Smith." *The Quarterly Journal of Economics* 69, no. 2 (1955): 161–90.

———. "The Concept of the Just Price: Theory and Economic Policy." *The Journal of Economic History* 18, no. 4 (1958): 418–34.

Rothbard, Murray N. *An Austrian Perspective on the History of Economic Thought*. Volume 1. Auburn, Alabama: Ludwig von Mises Institute, 2006.

Rubin, Jared. "Institutions, the Rise of Commerce and the Persistence of Laws: Interest Restrictions in Islam and Christianity." *The Economic Journal* 121, no. 557 (2011): 1310–39.

Schumpeter, Joseph Alois. *The History of Economic Analysis*. [n.p.]: [n.pub.], 1943.

Slavery Convention, 60 LNTS 253 § (1926).

Smith, Adam. *The Wealth of Nations*. Middlesex, England: Penguin Books Ltd., 1982.

St. Augustine. *Nicene and Post Nicene Fathers.* Vol. 8. Christian Classics Ethereal Library, Series I. Edited by Philip Schaff. Grand Rapids, MI: Christian Classics Ethereal Library, n.d.

Tanner, Norman P., ed. *Decrees of the Ecumenical Councils: Volumes 1: Nicaea I to Lateran V.* Washington, DC: Georgetown University Press, 1990.

Tawney, R.H. *Religion and the Rise of Capitalism: A Historical Study.* Drayton, Middlesex: Penguin Books, 1937.

Tenney, Glen. "The Social Blessings of 'Usury.'" *Mises Daily Articles* (blog). Accessed 3 July 2021. https://mises.org/library/social-blessings-usury.

Turgot, Anne Robert Jacques. *The Turgot Collection: Writings, Speeches, and Letters of Anne Robert Jacques Turgot.* Edited by Gordon David. Auburn, Alabama: Ludwig von Mises Institute, 2011.

Watt, Lewis. *Usury in Catholic Theology.* Oxford: Catholic Social Guild, 1963.

Williams, C. "Slavery, II (and the Church)." In *New Catholic Encyclopaedia.* Vol. 13. Washington DC: Catholic University of America, 2003.

Woods, Thomas E., Jr. *The Church and the Market: A Catholic Defense of the Free Economy.* Lanham, MD: Lexington Books, 2015.

WORKS CONSULTED

"Pope Francis Condemns Usury — but What Is It? — Institute of Economic Affairs." Accessed 25 November 2023. https://iea.org.uk/pope-francis-condemns-usury-but-what-is-it/.

Anscombe, G.E.M. *Faith in a Hard Ground: Essays on Religion, Philosophy and Ethics.* Edited by Mary Geach and Luke Gormally. Exeter: Imprint Academic, 2008.

Aristotle. *The Nicomachean Ethics.* Translated by J.A.K. Thomson. London: Penguin, 2004.

Bell, Adrian R., Chris Brooks, and Tony K. Moore. "Interest in Medieval Accounts: Examples from England, 1272–1340." *History* 94, no. 316 (October 2009): 411–33.

Belloc, Hilaire. *An Essay on the Restoration of Property.* IHS Press, 2002.

Bolles, John Augustus. *A Treatise on Usury and Usury Laws.* University of Michigan Library, 2009.

Boyer, George R., and Robert S. Smith. "The Development of the Neoclassical Tradition in Labor Economics." *ILR Review* 54, no. 2 (January 2001): 199–223. https://doi.org/10.1177/001979390105400201.

Buchmann, John. "A Time for Reconsidering the Catholic Prohibition of Usury." *Church Life Journal*, June 14, 2021. https://churchlifejournal.nd.edu/articles/revisiting-the-catholic-prohibition-of-usury/.

Cajetan, Thomas. *On Exchange and Usury*. Acton Institute for the Study of Religion & Liberty, 2014.

Clary, Betsy Jane. "Institutional Usury and the Banks." *Review of Social Economy* 69, no. 4 (December 2011): 419–38.

Cooper, Ben. *The Ethics of Usury*. London: The Latimer Trust, 2012.

Coulter, Fr. Gary L. "The Church and Usury: Error, Change or Development?" A research paper, Mount Saint Mary's Seminary, 1999.

De Mariana, Juan, P.T. Brannan, Stephen J. Grabill, and Alejandro A. Chaufen. *A Treatise on the Alteration of Money*. Grand Rapids, Michigan: CLP Academic, 2011.

De Molina, Luis. *A Treatise on Money*. Translated by Jeannine Emery. Acton Institute for the Study of Religion & Liberty, 2015.

De Roover, Raymond. *The Rise and Decline of the Medici Bank: 1397–1494*. Cambridge, MA.: Harvard Univ. Press, 1963.

Decock, Wim. "Lessius and the Breakdown of the Scholastic Paradigm." *Journal of the History of Economic Thought* 31, no. 1 (2009): 57–78.

Gerardus, Senensis, and Lawrin D Armstrong. *The Idea of a Moral Economy: Gerard of Siena on Usury, Restitution, and Prescription*. Toronto: University Of Toronto Press, 2016.

Gilchrist, John Thomas. *The Church and Economic Activity in the Middle Ages*. London; Melbourne [etc.]: Macmillan; New York: St. Martin's Press, 1969.

Hayes, M.G. "Keynes's Liquidity Preference and the Usury Doctrine: Their Connection and Continuing Policy Relevance." *Review of Social Economy* 75, no. 4 (2017): 400–416.

Hayes, Mark. "Urgent Challenges for Christian Social Thought." In *An Ethical Debate on Finance and Technology*. London, 2019.

Herbener, Jeffrey M., ed. *The Pure Time-Preference Theory of Interest*. Auburn, Alabama: Ludwig von Mises Institute, 2011.

Hoffman, Michael A. *Usury in Christendom, the Mortal Sin That Was and Now Is Not: A Study of the Rise of the Money Power in the West*. Coeur d'Alene, ID: Independent History and Research, 2013.

Hume, David. *Of Money, and Other Economic Essays Illustrated*. Independently published, 2021.

Jones, E. Michael. *Doing Business with Strangers: Finance and Enterprise in the Preindustrial World*. South Bend, Indiana: Fidelity Press, 2014.

Kaelber, Lutz. "Financing Business: Max Weber on Equity and Debt in Medieval Commercial Partnerships." Yale University, 2015.

———. "Max Weber on Usury and Medieval Capitalism: From *The History of Commercial Partnerships* to *The Protestant Ethic*." *Max Weber Studies* 4, no. 1 (January 2004): 51–75.

Kelly, J. M. "A Hypothesis on the Origin of 'Mutuum.'" *Irish Jurist* 5, no. 1 (Summer 1970): 156–63.

Kerridge, Eric. *Usury, Interest, and the Reformation*. Ashgate Publishing, 2002.

Koyama, Mark. "Evading the 'Taint of Usury': The Usury Prohibition as a Barrier to Entry." *Explorations in Economic History*, 2010.

Kreikebaum, Hartmut, Hartwig Bechte, Theodor Ellinger, and Shael Herman. *Medieval Usury and the Commercialization of Feudal Bonds*. Vol. 11. Duncker & Humblot, 2021.

Lapidus, André. "Information and Risk in the Medieval Doctrine of Usury during the Thirteenth Century." *Perspectives on the History of Economic Thought* 5 (1991): 23–38.

Lawson, Tony, and Hashem Pesaran. *Keynes' Economics: Methodological Issues*. London: Routledge, 2009.

Lee, Joanne. "Should Interest Rates Be Regulated? The Case for the Abolition of Usury." *The Western Australian Jurist* 8 (2017): 227–62.

Lessius, Leonardus. *On Sale, Securities, and Insurance*. CLP Academic, 2016.

Lewison, Martin. "Conflicts of Interest? The Ethics of Usury." *Journal of Business Ethics* 22, no. 4 (December 1999): 327–39.

Long, D. Stephen. "Bernard Dempsey's Theological Economics: Usury, Profit, and Human Fulfillment." *Theological Studies* 57, no. 4 (1996): 690–706.

Maritain, Jacques. "A Society without Money." *Review of Social Economy* 43, no. 1 (1985): 73–83.

Mathiowetz, Dean. "The Juridical Subject of 'Interest.'" *Political Theory* 35, no. 4 (August 2007): 468–394.

McCall, Brian M. "Unprofitable Lending: Modern Credit Regulation and the Lost Theory of Usury." *Cardozo Law Review* 30 (2008): 549.

McLaughlin, Terence Patrick. "The Teaching of the Canonists of Usury." *Mediaeval Studies* 1 (1939): 81–147.

Monslave, Fabio. "Late Spanish Doctors on Usury, and the Evolving Scholastic Tradition." *Journal of the History of Economic Thought* 36, no. 2 (June 2014): 215–35.

Mooney, S. C. *Usury, Destroyer of Nations*. Warsaw, OH: Theopolis, 1988.

Murray, J. B. C. *The History of Usury, from the Earliest Period to the Present Time, Etc.* Philadelphia: J. B. Lippincott & Co., 1866.

Nelson, Benjamin. *The Idea of Usury: From Tribal Brotherhood to Universal Otherhood*. Chicago: University of Chicago Press, 1969.

Parsons, Anscar. "Economic Significance of the *Montes Pietatis*." *Franciscan Studies* 22 (September 1941): 3–28.

Rao, John C. *Luther and His Progeny: 500 Years of Protestantism and Its Consequences for Church, State, and Society*. Kettering, OH: Angelico Press, 2017.

Rothbard, Murray N. *Economic Controversies*. Ludwig von Mises Institute, 2011.

———. *The Mystery of Banking*. Auburn, Ala.: Ludwig Von Mises Institute, 2008.

Rose, H. Shields. *The Churches and Usury, Or, the Morality of Five per Cent*. London: T. Sealey Clark & Co., Ltd., 1910.

Schmoeckel, Mathias. "Johann Gerhard and the Good Use of Usury." *Journal of Markets & Morality* 22, no. 2 (2019): 544.

Sommerville, H. "Interest and Usury in a New Light." *The Economic Journal* 41, no. 164 (December 1931): 646–49.

Storck, Thomas. "Is Usury Still a Sin?" *Communio* 36 (Fall 2009): 447–74.

Styger, Paul. "Interest, Usury and Time: A Comment." *Koers* 58, no. 3 (n.d.): 375–81.

Taeusch, Carl F. "The Concept of 'Usury': The History of an Idea." *Journal of the History of Ideas* 3, no. 3 (June 1942): 291–318.

Tierney, Brian. *The Idea of Natural Rights*. Emory University Studies in Law and Religion, no. 5. Grand Rapids, Michigan: William B Eerdmans Publishing Company, 1997.
Trivellato, Francesca. *The Promise and Peril of Credit: What a Forgotten Legend about Jews and Finance Tells Us about the Making of European Commercial Society*. Princeton, New Jersey: Princeton University Press, 2021.
Van Houdt, Toon. "'Lack of Money': A Reappraisal of Lessius' Contribution to the Scholastic Analysis of Money-Lending and Interest-Taking." *The European Journal of the History of Economic Thought* 5, no. 1 (Spring 1998): 1–35.
Visser, Wayne A.M., and Alastair Macintosh. "A Short Review of the Historical Critique of Usury." *Accounting, Business & Financial History* 8, no. 2 (1 July 1998): 175–89.
Von Mises, Ludwig. *Treatise on Economics: Human Action*. Ludwig Von Mises Institute, 2010.
Watt, Lewis. *Usury in Catholic Theology*. The Catholic Social Guild, 1963.
Weber, Max. *The Protestant Ethic and the Spirit of Capitalism*. London: Unwin University Books, 1956.
Welsh, John. *A Few Practical Comments on the Usury Law*. Philadelphia: M'Calla & Stavely, 1873.
Wishloff, Jim. "Usury and the Common Good." *Journal of Vincentian Social Action* 3, no. 2 (2018).
Woodyard, William M. and Chad G. Marzen. "Is Greed Good? A Catholic Perspective on Modern Usury." *Brigham Young University Journal of Public Law* 27, no. 1 (January 2012): 185–228.
Wykes, Michael. "Devaluing the Scholastics: Calvin's Ethics of Usury." *Calvin Theological Journal* 38, no. 1 (2003): 27–51.
Zarlenga, Stephen. "A Brief History of Interest," 18 December 2010. https://monetary.org/articles/a-brief-history-of-interest/.
Zimmermann, Reinhard. *The Law of Obligations: Roman Foundations of the Civilian Tradition*. Oxford: Oxford University Press, 2013.

www.ingramcontent.com/pod-product-compliance
Lightning Source LLC
Chambersburg PA
CBHW030245010526
44107CB00031B/1335/J